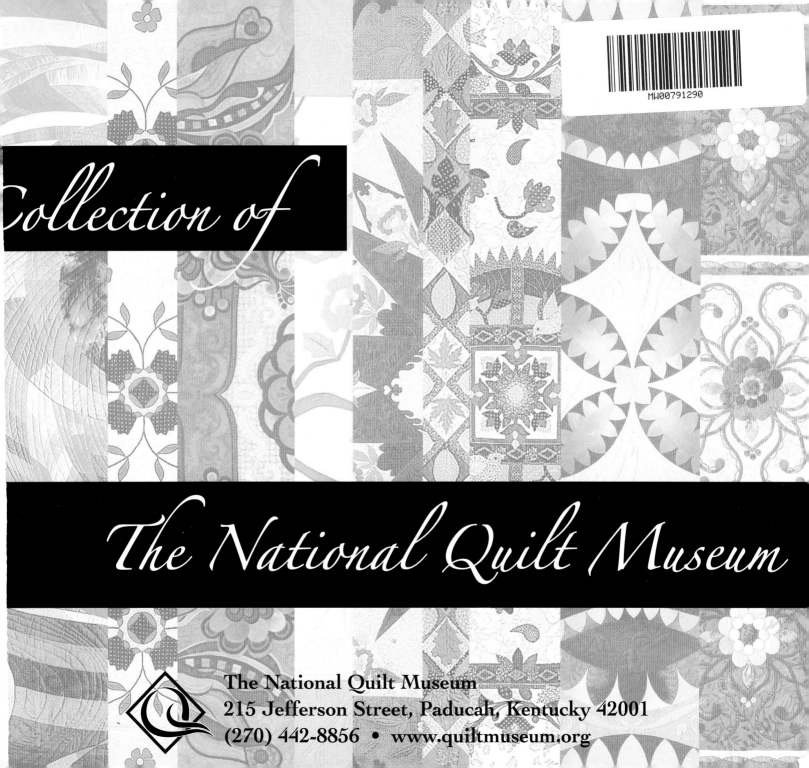

Collection of

The National Quilt Museum

The National Quilt Museum
215 Jefferson Street, Paducah, Kentucky 42001
(270) 442-8856 • www.quiltmuseum.org

ACKNOWLEDGMENTS

Great appreciation is due to
Charles R. Lynch for his excellent photography throughout the book,
to Judy Schwender, the Museum's Curator of Collections,
for the work of maintaining collection records,
to Andi Reynolds, for her assistance in collecting and editing information,
and to Angela Schade for graphic design.

Located in Paducah, Kentucky, the American Quilter's Society (AQS) is dedicated to promoting the accomplishments of today's quilters. Through its publications and events, AQS strives to honor today's quiltmakers and their work and to inspire future creativity and innovation in quiltmaking.

EXECUTIVE EDITOR: ANDI MILAM REYNOLDS
GRAPHIC DESIGN: ANGELA SCHADE
COVER DESIGN: ANGELA SCHADE
PHOTOGRAPHY: CHARLES R. LYNCH, UNLESS OTHERWISE NOTED

Additional copies of this book may be ordered from the American Quilter's Society, PO Box 3290, Paducah, KY 42002-3290; or online at www.AmericanQuilter.com; or from The National Quilt Museum, 215 Jefferson Street, Paducah, KY 42001, (270) 442-8856, www.quiltmuseum.org.

American Quilter's Society
P. O. Box 3290 • Paducah, KY 42002-3290
www.AmericanQuilter.com

Library of Congress Cataloging-in-Publication Data

National Quilt Museum.
   Collection of the National Quilt Museum / by the National Quilt Museum; Andi Reynolds, editor.
      p. cm.
   Includes index.
   ISBN 978-1-57432-987-2
   1. Quilts--United States--History--20th century--Catalogs. 2. Quilts--United States--History--21st century--Catalogs. 3. Quilts--Kentucky--Paducah--Catalogs. 4. National Quilt Museum--Catalogs. I. Reynolds, Andi Milam, 1953- II. Title.

   NK9112.N26 2009
   746.46074'76995--dc22

                              2009001831

Proudly printed and bound in the
United States of America

DEDICATION

This book is dedicated to
Bill and Meredith Schroeder.

Just as their vision and hard work have turned many dreams into reality, so have their admiration of quilts and support of today's quiltmakers advanced the art of quiltmaking.

Time and again Bill and Meredith have had a vision and brought it to fruition.

In 1984 they founded the American Quilter's Society, an international membership organization that began publishing *American Quilter* as a quarterly magazine. AQS membership has grown dramatically, and the magazine has become a bimonthly.

Publishing books on quiltmaking techniques and history followed. AQS is a leader and innovator in the field of "how-to" publishing in the quilt industry.

Another vision—to hold a yearly quilt show and contest in Paducah, Kentucky—was realized in 1985. With the growth and popularity of quilting worldwide, that dream has become three annual, international quilt shows in three locations.

In 1991 the Museum of the American Quilter's Society opened to exhibit contemporary quilts year round—a bold, visionary move. The museum's collections, which the Schroeders started with 85 quilts, have grown to over 300 quilts. In recognition of its cultural importance to the nation, in 2008 the United States Congress designated the museum that began as their idea as The National Quilt Museum of the United States.

Bill and Meredith Schroeder
Expanding the Vision, Advancing the Art

CONTENTS

Foreword by a Friend

Twenty-five years ago I was sitting at my desk in San Francisco. Paul Pilgrim, my partner, was thumbing through a magazine and said, "How would you like to do a quilt show in Paducah, Kentucky?" I said I wouldn't. He said, "Oh, come on, it could be fun."

It was not as if Paducah, Kentucky, was an unknown to us. Our good friend and head of the graduate department of Mills College, where we had both completed our master's degrees, was born in Paducah, so we knew something of the area.

Quilts were already an important part of our lives. We collected as well as bought and sold antique quilts for many years prior to our introduction to the new world of quilts we were about to discover.

Shows were also a familiar area to us because we had done many antique shows throughout the country as part of our antique business in California. However, our focus was the design business and I felt this quilt show thing would be a distraction. Needless to say I was convinced this would be like a vacation and the next thing I knew we were packed and in a rental car driving from St. Louis to Paducah.

As we approached Paducah I was impressed with the natural beauty of the area with its rivers, trees, and hills. When we drove into town, I immediately thought of all the romantic notions that southern writers have of describing sleepy river towns where time stands still and progress has given way to the past.

As we drove to the Executive Inn and saw the flood wall for the first time, I must confess I was a bit concerned. The Inn looked like a fortress and not knowing if the wall was to keep people in or out was puzzling. For those who did not see Paducah twenty-five years ago, you have no idea of the "draw" power there is in quilts. We nearly turned back.

That first show was an experience. We had designed a booth that fit our space and upon set up realized we were one of the only booths with antique quilts. We were amazed at the amount of merchandise related to sewing and specifically quiltmaking that was available. Here we were in our shirts, ties, and jackets surrounded by a whole new world we knew nothing about. As it turned out, two men in the quilt world stick out like sore thumbs anyway, so we thought, "What do we have to lose?"

On our first morning in Paducah, Paul and I were swimming laps in the hotel pool with one other person. That person was Katy Christopherson. She was a mover and a shaker in the quilt world and we soon became good friends. It was she who introduced us to Bill and Meredith Schroeder.

Through our involvement with AQS in the early years and the friendships we developed, a reciprocal relationship formed that combined our professional services along with personal pleasures. It has been a good fit.

In 1987 Meredith and Bill Schroeder announced that a non-profit quilt museum was to be built in Paducah to honor today's quilters. The quilt collection housed there was formed in a unique manner. Purchase award quilts, along with a collection of quilts Meredith and Bill Schroeder had privately purchased, began the AQS Quilt Collection and continue its growth. (Many of the quilts were accessed in 1997.)

The collection has continued to grow with each annual show, as has the tradition of prize winners. Prize-winning quilts in several of the categories from the annual contest can also be purchase awards—the quiltmaker has the choice of the prize money or the quilt. In addition, there is an effort on the part of the museum to select quilts to purchase in order to secure examples other than those submitted for competition. This practice ensures that the collection reflects not just variety but also the best.

I feel very fortunate that we were asked to be a part of the development of the museum project. Paul and I had, over the years, curated many exhibitions for museums and galleries using our collection and were very familiar with the specific need of textiles. We both came from fine art backgrounds and had many years of experience in the building and remodeling business through our design business in the San Francisco Bay Area.

Being avid museum goers, we felt perfectly confident in our abilities to take on the job. Our goal was to create a facility that was not only state of the art, but welcoming, friendly, and not forbidding. It was a dream come true in many ways. Working with Paul Gresham, a young, inspired, and passionate local architect, was a pleasure. Others we came to know well: Gerry Montgomery, former mayor and board member; Craig Guess, building contractor; Victoria Faoro, our first executive director; and, of course, the Schroeder family.

The Museum of the American Quilter's Society opened in 1991, the only facility of its kind designed specifically to show quilts as works of art. What an impact it has made, not only to the community, but to the quilt world in general.

One only needs to look at Paducah today to see the power of quilts. It is a community that has been reborn, rejuvenated, and restored through the efforts of creative and talented quiltmakers and by the dedication and dreams of a family who felt it was important to celebrate and reward those efforts. All those members of the community who worked so hard and for so long deserve to be very proud.

In 2008 the Congress of the United States designated a new, official name for the museum to reflect its importance on a national and international level. We are now The National Quilt Museum.

Gerald E. Roy
Paul D. Pilgrim / deceased 1996
Pilgrim / Roy

INTRODUCTION

The heart of The National Quilt Museum is informally known as the Founders' Collection. It highlights the works of contemporary quilters beginning in the 1980s through the twenty-first century to date. It shows the variety of quilting techniques and styles from hand to longarm machine quilting and from traditional patterns to computer-generated design and creative techniques. As a result, the collection continues both to document the changes in contemporary quilting today and to honor quiltmakers and their evolution as artists.

This collection is exhibited in the William and Meredith Schroeder Gallery and continues to grow. Through the annual acquisition of purchase award quilts from the American Quilter's Society Show & Contest in Paducah, Kentucky, the donation of quilts to the Museum by the makers or current owners, and the purchase of quilts selected by the Museum's Collections Committee, the collection continues to expand and keep current with the best work of today's quilters.

The AQS Show & Contest purchase awards presently include the American Quilter's Society Best of Show Quilt; AQS Hand Workmanship Award; Bernina Machine Workmanship Award; Gammill Longarm Machine Quilting Award; Moda Best Wall Quilt Award; and Benartex Best Miniature Award.

Award categories have changed over time to reflect quiltmaking evolution. Other award sponsors have included Gingher, Hancock's of Paducah, RJR, and Timeless Treasures.

Collection of The National Quilt Museum is the third publication to highlight the 234 quilts and 197 quiltmakers of this outstanding collection. This edition has a new format that showcases these amazing quilts by quiltmaker, presented alphabetically. Where possible, current artist statements introduce these talented artists, who were asked to answer the question, "What do you hope to achieve with the artistry of your quiltmaking?" For some quiltmakers, information was taken from the previous book, Web sites, and other sources. The awards listed were won at the American Quilter's Society Quilt Show & Contest in Paducah, Kentucky, unless otherwise noted. Honors such as being named a National Quilting Association Masterpiece Quilt or being named one of the 100 Best American Quilts of the 20th Century are also listed.

Additional Collections

The Museum now has three additional collections: the *Oh Wow!* Miniature Collection, *Blending the Old & the New: Quilts by Paul D. Pilgrim* Traveling Collection, and an Educational Collection used to explain and demonstrate the art of quilting. Together the Museum collections include more than 300 quilts.

Quilts in the Paul D. Pilgrim Traveling Collection are featured in the book *Blending the Old and the New*. This collection was developed as a tribute to the late Paul D. Pilgrim, a quiltmaker and quilt collector who, along with Gerald Roy, played an important role in the development of the Museum. This collection travels to museums throughout the United States.

The *Oh Wow!* Miniature Collection is on exhibit in the Museum's *Oh Wow!* Miniature Gallery. The first selection of miniature quilts is presented in both hardback and leather bound editions of *Oh Wow! The Miniature Quilts and Their Makers*. As this collection grows, some of its miniature quilts will continue to be exhibited in the Museum while others will travel.

Museum Activities

The Museum provides adult and youth workshops and activities that encourage the development of skills in the quilting arts. The Museum holds an annual contest, *New Quilts from an Old Favorite*, for quilts based on a traditional pattern but designed and made with a contemporary flair. The contest is sponsored by Clover Needlecraft, Fairfield Processing Corp., and Janome America, Inc. Winning quilts in the contest are exhibited at the Museum and are featured in a *New Quilts from an Old Favorite* book. Each exhibit then travels for two years throughout the country.

School Block Challenge is an annual contest for kindergarten through high school youth. Sponsored by Moda Fabrics, who provides the fabrics, the *School Block* contest challenges students to use three fabrics to express their creativity in a 16" quilt block. Winning schools are awarded prizes, students receive certificates, and all blocks entered in the contest are exhibited in the Museum.

The Museum offers ten to twelve gallery exhibits annually; they change every two to three months. More than 150 quilts are on exhibit at one time. In addition to the exhibit of quilts from the Museum's collections, the Museum curates a variety of exhibits available for view only at The National Quilt Museum. These vary from selections of contemporary quilters such as the recent *On a Grand Scale: Selections from Inge Mardal/Steen Hougs and Eleanor McCain;* and *Eyecatchers,* selections from the private collection of Robert and Barbara Hunter; to antique exhibits such as *Log Cabins and Lincoln* for the Abraham Lincoln Bicentennial. Recent traveling quilt exhibits hosted by the Museum included selections from Quilt National, Studio Art Quilters Associates, and 9th Quilt Japan.

The National Quilt Museum fulfills its mission to educate, promote, and honor today's quiltmaker by introducing the public to quilts exhibited as art in its galleries, and by providing excellent adult and youth workshops and programs. Since opening in 1991 as a non-profit institution, the Museum has shared extraordinary quilts, information, and inspiration with more than 675,000 visitors.

Support

The Museum is supported by donations, visitors, sponsors, and activities. Support also comes from the Kentucky Arts Council and federal funding from the National Endowment for the Arts. For addditional information, please call (270) 442-8856 or visit www.quiltmuseum.org.

GALLERIES

Quilts from the collection are always on display; a few are changed every two or three months. Visiting and special exhibit schedules may be seen on the Museum's Web site, www.quiltmuseum.org.

Collection of The National Quilt Museum

Special exhibits bring quilts from around the world to Paducah, such as "9th Quilt Japan," exhibited from July 11 to October 7, 2008, and "On a Grand Scale: Quilts by Steen Hougs, Inge Mardal & Eleanor McCain" exhibited August 16 to November 5, 2008.

Verla Hale
ADAMS & GOBLE
Mary Carol

Quilting was a matter of providing warmth and love for her family for Verla. It was also a family effort; for many years, she quilted "beautiful pieced tops" made by her daughter, Mary Carol Goble.

Verla Hale Adams

I hope to inspire people to try anything creative that will make them feel good about themselves. Quiltmaking has been a great comfort to me.

Mary Carol Goble

TRIP AROUND THE WORLD

105" x 108", Mary Carol Goble, Nephi, UT, and Verla Hale Adams, Oakley, ID, 1985. Cottons and cotton blends; machine pieced and hand quilted.
1997.06.86

Having learned how to make quilts from her Sioux in-laws, especially in the Broken Star pattern, Dawn found artistry and achievement later when she began dyeing her own fabrics.

THE BEGINNINGS
64" x 84", Dawn Amos, Rapid City, SD, 1990. Cottons, hand dyed; hand appliquéd and hand quilted.
1996.01.05

AWARDS:
AQS
Best of Show
1990

DAWN AMOS

DAWN AMOS

DESCENDING VISIONS
46" x 62", Dawn Amos, Rapid City, SD, 1992. Hand-dyed cottons; hand appliquéd and hand quilted.
1996.01.09

AWARDS:
RJR
Best Wall Quilt
1992

AWARDS:
RJR
Best Wall Quilt
1989

LOOKING BACK ON BROKEN PROMISES
53" x 38", Dawn Amos, Rapid City, SD, 1989. Cottons, hand dyed; hand appliquéd and hand quilted.
1996.01.16

Charlotte WARR ANDERSEN

Charlotte is best known for her highly realistic, original, unique pictorial quilts. A popular and effective teacher, she enjoys making quilts that connect with American history.

THREE FOR THE CROWN

54" x 54", Charlotte Warr Andersen, Salt Lake City, UT, 1987. Silks; hand pieced and hand quilted.
1997.06.83

The only reason I have ever made a quilt or other art work was to see how it would come out, to see if I had the skills to create what was in my mind's eye.

Each project would have to be challenging because if I were already certain of the outcome, it wouldn't be fun to make.

The surprises and discoveries of the creative process are the payoff, more so than the finished piece.

GARDEN PARTY
83" x 98.5", Faye Anderson, Boulder, CO, 1987. Cottons; machine pieced, hand appliquéd, hand embroidered, and hand quilted. 1992.05.01

FAYE ANDERSON

FAYE ANDERSON

SPRING WINDS
*76" x 87", Faye Anderson, Boulder,
CO, 1986. Cottons; hand appliquéd and
hand quilted.
1996.01.24*

AWARDS:
AQS
Best of Show
1986

Collection of The National Quilt Museum

Janice brings her painter's eye for color to her fabric choices. She finds artistry in the interplay of light and color and achievement in the technical challenges of good workmanship.

INCANTATION,
29" x 44", Janice Anthony, Jackson, ME, 1984. Cottons, painted silk; hand and machine pieced, and hand quilted.
1997.06.29

JANICE ANTHONY

VIRGINIA AVERY

When I started my career I simply wanted to make quilts and one-of-a-kind clothing well enough that I would be asked to teach.

I wanted my personal stamp on everything I made, and I wanted to help my students draw on their own resources—develop an idea or inspiration, choose the colors and techniques, and follow their own creativity in producing the very best work they could. When this has been accomplished, affirmation and satisfaction naturally follow.

Quiltmaking taxes creativity. We are somehow compelled to go through the "what if?" process to see what happens. Eventually, we leave our mark on line, function, form, color, and texture. There is endless excitement to this process and endless satisfaction in its completion.

MOVE OVER MATISSE I
36" x 70", Virginia Avery, Port Chester, NY, 1980.
Cottons; hand appliquéd and hand quilted.
2001.01.01

Iris is well-known for her leaf print quilts, wallhangings, and framed pieces. A member of the Southern Highland Craft Guild, she spends her time concentrating on creating her pieces. Hammering, dyeing, and weaving techniques inform the organic look of her work.

AWARDS:
RJR
Best Wall Quilt
1994

HAMMERED AT HOME

77" x 78", Iris Aycock, Woodville, AL, 1994. Cottons; machine pieced and machine quilted.
1996.01.13

BARBARA BARBER

The numerous challenges inherent in making quilts appeal to Barbara, whether working in a color unusual for her, entering a competition, or making a quilt within a certain time frame. Teaching others is a vital part of passing along her self-taught machine-quilting skills.

AWARDS:
*Bernina
Machine Workmanship*
1996

GOATO AND FRIENDS

83" x 83", Barbara Barber, Andover, Hants, England, 1995. Cottons; machine appliquéd, machine quilted, and machine embroidered.
1996.02.01

When talking about my work, I usually call myself a craftsperson using the medium of the quilt to create high-end, functional and/or decorative items.

It is imperative to please myself by making the very best technical and artistic statement possible no matter the material, be it hand-dyed cotton, recycled wool, or silk. The techniques that I use must allow me to achieve this goal.

I hope to seriously engage each viewer so that she or he experiences my work to the fullest. I also hope to inspire my viewers to create work that is gratifying to them.

SONYA LEE BARRINGTON

BED QUILT #1

87" x 92.5", Sonya Lee Barrington, San Francisco, CA, c. 1992.
2007.13.01

CLETHA BIRD

Inspired by Grace McCance Snyder's needlepoint-like FLOWER BASKET quilt, Cletha set out to make a one-of-a-kind quilt of her own.

"Had I known more about the challenges of quiltmaking, I am sure that I would not have tried that design!"—especially for a first quilt, which is what this work was.

FLOWER BASKET
96" x 104", Cletha Bird, Columbus, IN, 1987. Cottons and cotton blends; machine pieced and hand quilted.
1997.06.22

24

Except to aim for good design and color, there are no goals to my quiltmaking other than to satisfy my need for a creative outlet.

I've done the teaching, lectures, and shows. I've won many awards, but nothing achieves satisfaction like the joy of actually creating something tangible from that idea in your head.

GYPSY IN MY SOUL

66" x 84", Jane Blair, Wyomissing, PA, 1987. Cottons and cotton/polyesters; hand pieced, hand appliquéd, and hand quilted. Named one of the 100 Best American Quilts of the 20th Century. 1996.01.12

AWARDS:
AQS
Best of Show
1988

JANE BLAIR

JANE BLAIR

MORISCO
80" x 90", Jane Blair, Wyomissing, PA, 1984. Cottons and cotton/polyester blends; hand pieced and hand quilted. 1997.06.40

NIGHT BLOOM

56" x 72", Jane Blair, Wyomissing, PA,
1985. Cottons and cotton/polyesters; hand
pieced and hand quilted.
1997.06.46

AWARDS:
First Place
Wall Quilt, Professional
1986

JANE BLAIR

JANE BLAIR

RAGGEDY SUN WORSHIPPERS
48" x 64", Jane Blair, Wyomissing, PA, 1996. Cottons, cotton/polyesters; hand appliquéd, hand and machine pieced, and hand quilted.
1996.04.01

AWARDS:
RJR
Best Wall Quilt
1996

My quilts are visual diaries that reflect what I love and record what I remember. They are personal recollections in quilt form, expressed abstractly rather than pictorially.

So while my work contains allusions to content that may, at first, be meaningful only to me, I always hope that color and composition will somehow convey that content, in a way that will intrigue—or at least attract—the viewer's interest and appreciation.

What I hope to achieve is the empathy and involvement of viewers by evoking a response that allows them to discover their own meaning, that evokes a memory of their own, that inspires a kind of "conversation without words,"—a collaboration between the quiltmaker and the observer.

THE MOUNTAIN AND THE MAGIC: NIGHT LIGHTS

65" x 65", Judi Warren Blaydon, Milford, MI, 1995. Lamé, rayon, American and Japanese cottons, antique kimono silk; machine pieced, hand quilted, hand appliquéd, and hand beaded.
2001.02.01

JUDI WARREN BLAYDON

ARLEEN BOYD

ROSES BY STARLIGHT
89" x 100.5", Arleen Boyd, Rochester, NY, 1985. Cottons; machine pieced and hand quilted.
1997.06.66

Quiltmaking offers the opportunity to combine comfort with artistry.

My first introduction to it was in visiting my prospective in-laws in Pennsylvania. They were prime examples of thrift and made quilts for use, but as lovely as possible with what they had on hand, usually scraps from home sewing.

Now that we are grandparents there are added opportunities to supply quilts for cuddling, which provides pleasure in the making and in seeing them used.

Because of the friendships formed in quilt clubs and at shows, my life is enriched by sharing ideas and working with others who enjoy the same activity.

I was born to sew and quilt. Quiltmaking is the creative outlet to explore the endless design and color ideas I have, to experiment with and learn from as my ideas grow.

It's more than just the design and the color; the hand quilting soothes my soul and frees my mind.

Over the decades I have achieved recognition and numerous awards, which validate my quilts; however my greatest achievements in quiltmaking are the many friends that I have made along the way and knowing that my children and grandchildren sleep under quilts stitched with love, just the way I did when I was a child.

AWARDS:
First Place
Innovative Pieced, Professional
1995

DREAMCATCHER
66" x 82", Becky Brown, Richmond, VA, 1994. Cottons; hand pieced, hand appliquéd, hand quilted.
1997.07.08

NANCY S. BROWN

Ultimately, I hope that my quilts will be around for a long time and will become a part of how I leave my mark on this earth.

As for right now, I hope that both my family and animal quilts bring some enjoyment to their viewers.

I also hope that my animal quilts help their viewers become more aware of the beauty and importance of animals in this world.

AWARDS:
RJR
Best Wall Quilt
1993

MOUNT PLEASANT MINERS
48" x 55", Nancy S. Brown, Oakland, CA, 1993. Cottons, hand dyed and painted; hand appliquéd, machine pieced, and hand quilted.
1996.01.20

I have been quilting for thirty years, but my love of needlework and sewing began as a small child using my mother's treadle sewing machine. From making Christmas ornaments to my first formal sewing instruction to completing my first quilt in the 1970s, I have enjoyed every part of the process—designing, choosing fabrics, stitching, and completing the projects.

As a visual person, I see quilt patterns and quilting designs everywhere that I travel. My inspiration comes from a field of wild flowers, clouds in the sky, or the birds in our backyard. With photography as my hobby, I am known to record hundreds of photographs during my trips to use as design sources in my work.

AWARDS:
Third Place Award
Other Techniques, Amateur
1986

BONNIE K. BROWNING

A LITTLE BIT OF CANDLEWICKING
64" x 97", Bonnie K. Browning, Paducah, KY, 1983. Unbleached muslin, Cluny lace and satin ribbon; candlewicked, machine pieced, and hand quilted. 1997.06.33

BARBARA BRUNNER

Barbara creates virtual flower gardens by making roses and tulips come alive in her quilt art.

Quilting is how she expresses her feelings and ideas, and she tries to quilt every day.

ROSES FOR A JUNE BRIDE
84" x 109", Barbara Brunner, Schofield, WI, 1986. Cottons; hand appliquéd and hand quilted.
1997.06.67

CYNTHIA BUETTNER

CROSSINGS
64" x 52", Cynthia Buettner, Hilliard, OH, 1986.
Hand-dyed cottons; machine pieced and hand quilted.
1997.06.15

With a great-grandmother described as a master quilter, Cynthia grew up fascinated by quilts. She has taught, designed her own fabrics, and sold hand-dyed fabrics around the world.

MONECA CALVERT

Moneca's designs and work-manship are recognized world-wide, and she has traveled the globe teaching contemporary quiltmaking for almost three decades.

NEON NIGHTS

53" x 53", Moneca Calvert, Reno, NV, 1986. Cottons, cotton blends; machine pieced and hand quilted.
1997.06.43

I love to make traditional quilts with contemporary twists. The twist may come from using new color combinations, or from adding a little appliqué or paint to traditional pieced blocks.

Most recently, I've discovered that simple blocks are more versatile than complicated ones. By utilizing highly contrasting fabrics or more subtle color and value changes, it is surprising the number of different ways there are to combine simple, traditional blocks.

My favorite part of the process, however, has always been the quilting. It is the "icing on the cake." I love designing the quilting motifs to fill the quieter spaces on the quilt's surface with texture. And I love the meditative nature of the actual quilting stitches, whether made by hand or by machine.

AWARDS:
AQS
Best Hand Workmanship
2003

STAR FLOWER

83" x 83", Elsie M. Campbell, Dodge City, KS, 2002. Cottons; machine pieced, machine appliquéd, and hand quilted. National Quilting Association Masterpiece Quilt.
2003.03.01

ELSIE M. CAMPBELL

Canyon Quilters of SAN DIEGO

O Our purpose "is to promote good fellowship among persons interested in the art of quiltmaking and to promote the knowledge and appreciation of all aspects of quiltmaking."

Working on donation projects such as this one provides our members with a great sense of satisfaction.

POPPIES AND OTHER CALIFORNIA BEAUTIES
88" x 112", Canyon Quilters of San Diego, San Diego, CA, 1991. Cottons; hand appliquéd, hand embroidered, and hand quilted. 1992.20.01

38

Collection of The National Quilt Museum

A passion for creating something of substance from raw materials led me to quilting.

It is this same "making" that has helped me find the strength and resiliency to be found in what is sensitive and fragile. I want to portray the poetry in the visual.

These early works are an attempt to manage (I no longer want to use the word "control") chaos, as portrayed by my use of color.

FREEDOM'S CASCADE

44" x 66", Erika Carter, Bellevue, WA, 1990. Cottons; machine pieced, hand appliquéd, and hand quilted.
1997.06.24

ERIKA CARTER

ERIKA CARTER

GRACE
45" x 69", Erika Carter, Bellevue, WA, 1993. Hand painted and commercial cottons; machine appliquéd and machine quilted.
1997.07.11

SUBMERGENCE

71" x 53", Erika Carter, Bellevue, WA, 1989. Cottons; machine pieced, hand appliquéd, and hand quilted.
1997.06.79

MARY CHARTIER

Mary believes quiltmakers should make work that suits themselves. She personally does better technical work if she knows it will be judged, but choices of design, color, and fabric should be governed by the individual's preferences.

MORNING GLORY

80" x 100", Mary Chartier, New London, CT, 1986. Cottons; hand appliquéd, hand and machine pieced, and hand quilted. 1992.17.01

AWARDS:
Second Place
Appliqué, Professional
1988

NANCY CLARK

PHOENIX RISING
95.5" x 80", Nancy Clark, Phoenix, AZ, 1987.
Cottons; machine pieced, hand appliquéd, hand painted, and hand quilted.
1997.06.56

Nancy's work has been inspired and informed by the intersection of childhood memories of the Arizona desert, dairy farming, veterinary medicine, and time spent in cities and suits.

BARBARA L. CRANE

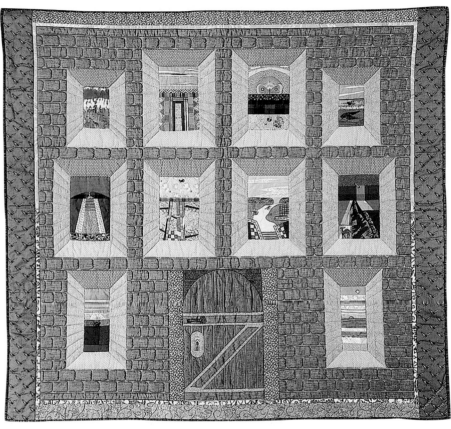

OUTLOOKS
58" x 51", Barbara L. Crane, Lexington, MA, 1984. Cottons and cotton blends; hand pieced, machine pieced, hand quilted, and embellished with small objects.
1997.06.53

AWARDS:
Third Place Wall Quilts, Amateur
1985

I hope my fabric landscapes suggest a sense of magic realism.

I try to create surprise and predictability at the same time, to reflect my wonder and appreciation of the natural world. I often use hand-dyed and hand-painted fabrics to suggest sky and water, and to create illusions of light and shadow.

Transformation is a favorite magical tool: scraps of old plaid shirts turn into farmers' fields; pale calicoes resemble distant flower patches; batiks, cut just right, become snowy ridges, gnarled tree limbs, and birds' beaks.

Quilting lines are transformable, as well, into furrows, flight lines of birds, water currents, and the swirl of the wind. Meticulous hand quilting supports one of my personal goals—to find a place of stillness in myself.

Before she passed away, a love of paper dolls and learning to quilt early from her mother guided Laura's design and quilt-making efforts.

UP, UP, AND AWAY
79" x 79", Laura Crews-Lewis, Cape Girardeau, MO, 1983. Cottons, chintz; hand appliquéd, hand quilted, stuffed, and Seminole pieced.
1997.06.89

LAURA CREWS-LEWIS

MARY JO DALRYMPLE

Aside from using up my pile of fabric and having done a lot of thinking while making quilts, I would hope that one achievement has been that others have shared my joy in the process.

ROCOCO ISLANDS
94" x 94", Mary Jo Dalrymple, Omaha, NE, 1982. Cottons; hand pieced and hand quilted.
1993.01.01

46

The creation of quilts using Francelise's "silkollage" technique involves layering silks, appliqué, painting, embroidery, and machine quilting. Exhibited and published nationally, she teaches her collage technique via lectures.

DISCOVERY

18.5" diameter, Francelise Dawkins, Queensbury, NY, 1991. Silks; machine appliquéd, machine embroidered, and machine quilted.
1997.07.07

FRANCELISE DAWKINS

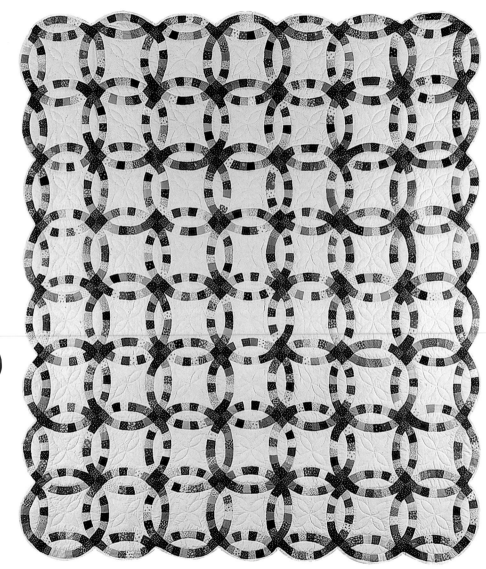

CLAUDIA DAWSON

Quiltmaking for Claudia evolved from something she watched her mother do to a fulfilling pastime pursued while her husband was working away from home.

DOUBLE WEDDING RING
93" x 108", Claudia Dawson, Harviell, MO, 1985. Cottons, cotton polyester blends; machine pieced and hand quilted. 1997.06.18

48

A pioneer quilting instructor in Holland, Hanne discovered quilting on a vacation in Vermont and learned how to quilt from Sophie Campbell in Paris.

STELLA ANTIGUA
91" x 91", Hanne Vibeke de Koning-Stapel, Bilthoven, Holland, 1988. Silks; hand pieced and hand quilted.
1993.03.01

AWARDS:
First Place
Traditional Pieced, Professional
1989

Hanne Vibeke
de KONING-STAPEL

JO DIGGS

SNOW SCAPE
72" x 62", Jo Diggs, Portland, ME, c. 1995. Wools;
machine pieced, hand appliquéd and quilted.
2004.02.01

*S*ewing and maintaining an avid
interest in art have fueled the creativity
in Jo's landscape quilts and her passion
for teaching over several decades.

Collection of The National Quilt Museum

According to her son, the late Adabelle had more ideas than time when it came to putting her ideas into quilts, even though she stretched the days by quilting in kerosene lamp light.

AWARDS:
First Place
Pictorial Wall Quilt
1990

ADABELLE DREMANN

CORN CRIB
42" x 47", Adabelle Dremann, Princeton, IL, 1989. Cottons; machine pieced, hand appliquéd, hand embroidered, and hand quilted with trapunto.
1997.06.13

ADABELLE DREMANN

COUNTRY SCHOOL
73" x 92", Adabelle Dremann, Princeton, IL, 1988. Cottons; machine pieced, hand appliquéd, and hand quilted.
1992.01.01

AWARDS:
Second Place
Appliqué, Amateur
1989

*B*eing the only person in my family who loved to sew, all I really wanted to do was learn to make a nice quilt. Eventually I did.

Then, I loved to share my ideas with those around me who made quilts, so I began to teach quiltmaking.

Now, many years later, I still teach a little. I just want to design and make my own quilts and the embroidered pieces I love, share them on my blog, and sometimes even sell a piece or two. It's fun and a great way to share what I love to do with people all over the planet.

I continue to learn and I'm still thrilled with the magic of what can be done with a needle and thread!

Patricia Eaton

*I*mmersion in almost every aspect of the quilt industry has influenced Donna's approach to quiltmaking.

Donna Fite McConnell

Patricia EATON & Donna Fite MCCONNELL

OUR SECRET GARDEN

87" x 87", Patricia Eaton and Donna Fite McConnell, Searcy, AR, 1990. Cottons; machine pieced, hand appliquéd, and hand quilted.
1997.06.52

CHRIS WOLF EDMONDS

Inspiration for her artistry has come to Chris via the expanse of the prairie, devoid of visual distraction but abundant with color and texture.

TREES: SUMMER/WINTER

41" x 51", Chris Wolf Edmonds, Lawrence, KS, 1999. Cotton, water-based pigments; hand painted and printed, machine pieced, and machine quilted. 2001.03.01

B. J.'s quilts are known for their pictorial qualities, to which she brings a folk-art perspective.

AWARDS:
First Place
Appliqué, Professional
1985

B. J. ELVGREN

TWELVE DAYS OF CHRISTMAS

102" x 108", B. J. Elvgren, Chesapeake, VA, 1983. Cottons, velvets, and silks; hand appliquéd, hand quilted with trapunto, and hand embroidered.
1997.06.88

LINDA GOODMON EMERY

For Linda, the definition of achieving quilt artistry is to set high goals and pursue them persistently.

ROSEMALING INSPIRATION

81" x 95", Linda Goodmon Emery, Derby, KS, 1986. Cottons and flexible ribbon floss embellishment; hand appliquéd and hand quilted. National Quilting Association Masterpiece Quilt.
1997.06.65

AWARDS:
Second Place
Appliqué, Professional
1986

As a quiltmaker, I work with enthusiasm and patience, drawing from experiences and things imagined.

Inspiration comes from within and from the observation of color, light, line, form, texture, and pattern on faces, figures, ordinary things, and in nature.

I strive for a high level of technical skill in hand appliqué, reverse appliqué, hand quilting, machine piecing, machine quilting, embellishing, and painting.

Jean M. Evans

My greatest joy in quiltmaking is the challenge—met head on and accomplished.

Now I have the freedom to be creative, to think and design artistically, and in the end, to make quilts from my own designs that are complex yet visually uncomplicated; still challenging; sometimes surprising; and for many reasons, pleasing to me.

Joyce Murrin

Jean M. Joyce
EVANS & MURRIN

MAY SHADOWS

60" x 60", Jean M. Evans, Medina, OH, and Joyce Murrin, Orient, NY, 1985. Cottons, cotton blends; hand appliquéd and hand quilted.
1997.06.39

CARYL BRYER FALLERT

BIRDS OF A DIFFERENT COLOR
74" x 93", Caryl Bryer Fallert, Oswego, IL, 1999. Hand-dyed cottons; machine pieced and machine quilted.
2000.01.01

The focus of my work is on the qualities of color, line, and texture, which engage the spirit and emotions of the viewer, evoking a sense of mystery, excitement, or joy inspired by visual impressions, collected in my travels, in my everyday life, and in my imagination.

Illusions of movement, depth, and luminosity are common to most of my work.

My quilts are about seeing, experiencing, and imagining, rather than pictorial representation of any specific object or species. When recognizable objects appear, they represent the emotions and flights of fantasy evoked by those objects.

I intend for my quilts to be seen and enjoyed by others. It is my hope that they will lift the spirits and delight the eyes of those who see them.

AWARDS:
Hancock's of Paducah
Best of Show
2000

Collection of The National Quilt Museum

CORONA II: SOLAR ECLIPSE

76" x 94," Caryl Bryer Fallert, Oswego, IL, 1989. Hand-dyed fabrics; machine pieced and machine quilted. Named one of the 100 Best American Quilts of the 20th Century. 1996.01.07

AWARDS:
AQS
Best of Show
1989

CARYL BRYER FALLERT

CARYL BRYER FALLERT

MIGRATION #2
88" x 88", Caryl Bryer Fallert,
Oswego, IL, 1995. Cottons; dye
painted, hand dyed, machine
pieced, machine appliquéd, and
machine quilted.
1996.01.18

AWARDS:
AQS
Best of Show
1995

RED POPPIES
72" x 90", Caryl Bryer Fallert,
Oswego, IL, 1983. Cottons; machine
pieced and hand quilted.
1997.06.62

CARYL BRYER FALLERT

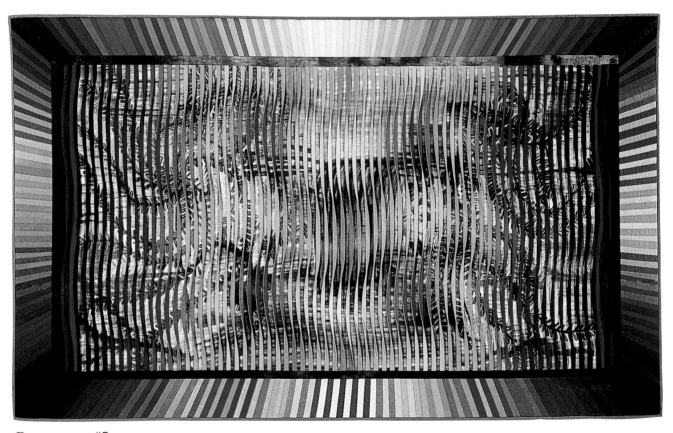

REFLECTION #3

77" x 45", Caryl Bryer Fallert, Oswego, IL, 1990. Hand-dyed, hand-painted fabrics; machine pieced and machine quilted.
1997.07.15

I wanted to leave to the quilt world and my family footprints of my passing and knowledge of the arts illustrated in stitches.

I accomplished this by having three quilts with permanent homes in museums. One is in the Gerald R. Ford Museum in Grand Rapids, Michigan; one is in the History and Culture Center in Charleston, West Virginia; and one is in the [formerly] Museum of the American Quilter's Society in Paducah, Kentucky.

I am now 82 years old, very proud to have accomplished my mission, and to all of you out there for giving me the opportunity to achieve my goals, thank you.

HAZEL B. REED FERRELL

NATURE'S WALK
99" x 103", Hazel B. Reed Ferrell, Middlebourne, WV, 1983. Cotton blends; hand appliquéd and hand quilted.
1997.06.41

DOROTHY FINLEY

DOT'S VINTAGE 1983

84" x 100", Dorothy Finley, Cordova, TN, 1983. Cottons; hand appliquéd and hand quilted with trapunto. National Quilting Association Masterpiece Quilt.
1996.01.10

One day Dorothy's husband came home with some quilt books belonging to one of his co-workers. He thought the quilts in the books were something else. To appease him, Dot, as she was known, began looking through one of them. She kept looking and looking and was amazed at what she saw. So she decided to make quilts.

Dot would never let anyone see what she was currently working on. That way, no one else would start working on that same pattern.

She loved genealogy and the old quilts, and that's what she wanted to do—pass on the old patterns and designs so people can know and love them as she did.

From a phone conversation with the late Dorothy Finley on 12/30/2008—Judy Schwender, TNQM Curator

AWARDS:
Gingher
Hand Workmanship Award
1985

Collection of The National Quilt Museum

We have loved quiltmaking ever since we learned how in the 1970s. Our designs have always been geared for mainstream quilters and presented to them through our books; our magazine, *Love of Quilting;* and our television programs on public TV.

Often inspired by the works of anonymous nineteenth- and early twentieth- century American quilters, we enjoy simplifying and updating basic techniques in order to make projects easy and accessible for today's hobby quilters.

STARS & STRIPES

80" x 96", Marianne Fons and Liz Porter, Winterset, IA, 2001. Machine pieced; machine quilted by Jean Nolte.
2007.04.01

Marianne **FONS** Liz **& PORTER**

Donna Duchesne
GAROFALO

Donna combined love of family, painting, and sewing into a lucrative, expressive quilting practice.

SERENITY II: LIFE IN MY POND
42" x 57", Donna Duchesne Garofalo, North Windham, CT, 1985. Cottons, cotton blends; machine pieced, hand quilted, and hand appliquéd.
1997.06.69

My vision is to create traditional quilts that transcend method, resulting in quilts with beautiful, interesting visual design, dimension, and purpose.

I work within a defined framework of tradition using a muted, sophisticated color palette, creating a fresh perspective from a modern vantage point.

My quilts are designed as I see them in my mind's eye; they are the quilts of today, using today's tools, a "new" tradition, but honoring and reflecting quilts of the past.

Quilting on my home sewing machine, I move the quilt under a carefully controlled needle to get precision, delicacy, and pleasing flow. I consider machine quilting fine needlework that refines and reflects the art and beauty of quilting as part of a long history of decorative arts.

AWARDS:
Bernina
Machine Workmanship
1999

BUTTERNUT SUMMER
81" x 81", Diane Gaudynski, Pewaukee, WI, 1998. Cottons; machine pieced and machine quilted. 1999.02.01

DIANE GAUDYNSKI

KETTLE MORAINE STAR
91" x 91", Diane Gaudynski, Pewaukee,
WI, 1996. Cottons; machine pieced and
machine quilted.
1997.02.01

AWARDS:
Bernina
Machine Workmanship
1997

Collection of The National Quilt Museum

OCTOBER MORNING
82" x 82", Diane Gaudynski,
Pewaukee, WI, 1999. Cottons;
machine pieced, machine quilted
with trapunto, and machine
broderie perse.
2000.03.01

AWARDS:
Bernina
Machine Workmanship
2000

DIANE GAUDYNSKI

DIANE GAUDYNSKI

SHADOWS OF UMBRIA
83" x 83", Diane Gaudynski, Waukesha, WI, 2006. Cottons, silk dupioni; machine pieced and quilted.
2008.05.01

AWARDS:
Bernina
Machine Workmanship
2008

SWEETHEART ON PARADE
82.5" x 83", Diane Gaudynski,
Pewaukee, WI, 1997. Cottons;
machine pieced and machine
quilted.
1998.03.01

AWARDS:
Bernina
Machine Workmanship
1998

DIANE GAUDYNSKI

CANDY GOFF

JOIE DE VIE – JOY OF LIFE
94" x 94", Candy Goff, Lolo, MT, 1998. Cottons; hand pieced, hand appliquéd, and hand quilted. Named one of the 100 Best American Quilts of the 20th Century.
1999.01.01

I hope to achieve a connection to the history and tradition of quiltmaking.

Today's cutting-edge quilts have examples of techniques used in antique quilts that we now perceive as innovative.

I often use antique quilts as inspiration to make an original design. To keep the traditional style of quiltmaking a viable art, I think it's important to maintain the creativity that was prevalent in early quilts. No two were the same.

My quilts are done entirely "by hand." This allows many hours of creative decision making as the design progresses. I enjoy the tactile feel of the fabric and quilt sandwich in my hands as the quilt nears completion.

I hope to continue the traditional quilt as an art form for the future.

AWARDS:
Hancock's of Paducah
Best of Show
1999

I have two quilts in museums and at my age I would just like to finish the quilts I have started.

I will always quilt, however; I think it's in my blood.

I am so thankful for my mother making me help her do the quilting. Every winter she would have one [quilt] in the frame. I have acquired some 1930-40 quilt tops, so I have been working on them.

FEATHERED STAR SAMPLER
97" x 97", Imogene Gooch, Rockville, IN, 1983. Cottons; hand pieced and hand quilted.
1997.06.21

AWARDS:
Second Place
Patchwork, Professional
1985

IMOGENE GOOCH

IRENE GOODRICH

What I hope to achieve with the artistry of my quiltmaking is difficult for me to answer as I'm in my eighties and a much better quilter than a writer!

To me quilting is a soothing, rewarding therapeutic experience. Beginning in 1970 I was a caregiver for several family members. During all the difficult times, prayers and quilting kept me sane. So to you quilters out there, should you find yourself in the same situation, keep on quilting!

I feel that quilting has helped me reach my older age and it is my hope that I will be able to add many more years to my age with my love of quilting.

LANCASTER COUNTY ROSE
90" x 110", Irene Goodrich, Columbus, OH, 1980. Cottons and cotton blends; hand pieced and hand quilted.
1997.06.31

My art emerges from my meditation practices and reflects my desire to explore the mystery of consciousness—that field of awareness that permeates and gives meaning to the universe.

My work explores those edges where science and spirituality come together as I play with my understanding in both quantum physics and spiritual inquiry, knowing that they both point to the same truth of oneness.

I create as a meditative practice, opening to the stillness in each moment, engaging the intelligence of my heart, becoming one with the flow of creativity.

This practice strengthens my ability to experience the beauty of deep presence in every moment of my life, to move with grace through difficult times, and to help others do the same.

AWARDS:

RJR

Best Wall Quilt

1991

Collection of The National Quilt Museum

ANCIENT DIRECTIONS

80" x 67," Alison Goss, Durango, CO, 1991. Cottons; machine pieced and machine quilted. Named one of the 100 Best American Quilts of the 20th Century.
1996.01.02

ALISON GOSS

ALISON GOSS

RESTORING THE BALANCE
95" x 80", Alison Goss, Durango, CO, 1990. Cottons and poly-cotton blends; machine pieced and hand quilted.
1992.08.01

I hope to convince all of my students and readers that there is no limit to what they can make with fabric.

All that is required is an inspiration, a desire, and an open-minded, inquisitive approach to techniques one has not tried.

Excitement, pleasure, and satisfaction await the person willing to try a new method, practice it, and apply it in a new way to his or her ideas.

FEAR OF THE DARK
87" x 87", Mary L. Hackett, Carterville, IL, 1993. Cottons; machine pieced and machine quilted.
1997.07.10

MARY L.HACKETT

JANE HALL

I hope to make quilts in the best tradition of the quiltmaker's art. I want the colors and the design to "sing," both for me and for the viewer. My quilts are most often fabric or color inspired, although sometimes I am influenced by the designs in antique quilts.

I enjoy exploring traditional patterns, especially in the Log Cabin/Pineapple family, with contemporary coloration and innovative tweaks and an occasional element of unpredictability.

The entire process of planning, designing, and constructing the quilt has a twofold meaning for me: it is a wonderfully satisfying tactile art form, and, at the same time, I have the sense of following in our foremothers' footsteps, making *woman's art.*

PINEAPPLE LOG CABIN
50" x 68", Jane Hall, Raleigh, NC, 1985. Cottons; machine pieced and hand quilted.
1997.06.57

Following my training and practice as a research scientist, my approach to quilting is decidedly experimental.

As scientists seek for truth and understanding in small, well-defined inquiries, quilters may piece together bits and pieces into an artistic theory of life.

My quilts are autobiographical in that real life issues are always represented in the overriding themes of the work, although it may not be recognizable to anyone other than myself. Indeed, the generation of real life solutions seems intimately connected to resolutions of artistic and technical problems during the art process.

As I work, I disassemble a problem and reassemble a solution, both in the quilt and in life. The name of any piece can immediately pinpoint a date, location, and concern in my memory.

AWARDS:

Bernina
Machine Workmanship
2001

VICKIE HALLMARK

ENLIGHTENMENT

85" x 85", Vicki Hallmark, Austin, TX, 2000. Cottons; polyester and metallic threads; machine pieced, machine appliquéd, and machine quilted.
2001.11.01

OLDE ENGLISH MEDALLION
104" x 104", Cindy Vermillion Hamilton, Pagosa Springs, CO, 1992. Cottons; hand pieced, hand appliquéd, and hand quilted.
1992.22.01

My reasons, methods, and interests in making quilts have changed little since the 1960s, when I was swept into the fascinating world of creating beautiful quilts.

As a history lover, I enjoy mentally traveling to times past as I hand stitch classic patterns, colors, and fabric styles into new arrangements that lift my spirit and make my soul sing.

I build my quilts upon recognizable elements and motifs that women of the past created. This allows me to be part of the wide world of female energy and imagery that has been captured and lovingly passed down to us through stitches.

I hope my quilts inspire others to be part of this journey that captures time.

AWARDS:
First Place
Traditional Pieced, Professional
1992

Collection of The National Quilt Museum

My goal is to merge my love of creating art using digital media with my love of quiltmaking to create work that pays respect to tradition while pushing its boundaries into tomorrow's possibilities.

I hope my quilt art first grabs the attention of the viewer and then draws the viewer in, evoking a sense of wonder.

Rather than the viewer being intrigued with the how, I'd rather the viewer enjoy the visual experience and contemplate the why.

AWARDS:
Moda
Best Wall Quilt
2008

GLORIA HANSEN

BLUSHING TRIANGLES 3

41.5" x 42", Gloria Hansen, East Windsor, NJ, 2008. Original digital painting; printed, painted, machine pieced and quilted.
2008.06.01

IRMA GAIL HATCHER

Hand workmanship, three-dimensional applique, and a love of flowers are the foundations of Irma Gail's artistry and achievements.

AWARDS:
Gingher
Hand Workmanship
1994

CONWAY ALBUM (I'M NOT FROM BALTIMORE)
86" x 89", Irma Gail Hatcher, Conway, AR, 1992. Cottons; hand appliquéd and hand quilted. Named one of the 100 Best American Quilts of the 20th Century.
1996.01.06

GARDEN MAZE
82" x 82", Irma Gail Hatcher, Conway,
AR, 1998. Cottons; machine pieced,
hand appliquéd, and hand quilted with
trapunto.
2000.02.01

AWARDS:
Timeless Treasures
Hand Workmanship
2000

IRMA GAIL HATCHER

DENISE TALLON HAVLAN

MUSES FOR A MILLENNIUM

72" x 80", Denise Tallon Havlan, Plainfield, IL, 2000. Cotton and synthetic commercial fabrics, textile paints and inks, Prismacolor® pencils; cotton, rayon, and metallic threads; hand and machine appliqué, fused; embellished, machine quilted.
2007.12.01

Seeing Amish quilts and falling in love with them, I entered the world of quiltmaking with very little sewing experience but a great willingness to learn.

In time I moved into the "art quilt" arena and let my imagination go. My intentions and goals are always directed toward creating one-of-a-kind images that portray the natural world and the people who inhabit it.

My ultimate purpose is to be part of leaving a legacy of how the beautiful and purposeful craft of quiltmaking continues to evolve with each generation's vision. Whether using traditional designs handed down from our ancestors or discovering new paths untraveled, we are keeping the art of the quilt alive forever!

AWARDS:
2nd Place
AQS Quilt Exposition,
Nashville, Tennessee
2000

Collection of The National Quilt Museum

I have been teaching and quilting professionally for more than 15 years and have developed a deep love and fascination with color and texture.

In quilting, it is the creative process that fascinates me, from concept through execution. I love the texture of the medium and the ability to express my artistic ideas through every step of the quilting process.

I am inspired by each aspect, from designing the fabrics, threads, and patterns on through the free-motion surface embellishment, quilting, and over-quilting elements.

It is my hope that my artistic expression through quilting will serve as inspiration for new quilters to discover their own talent hidden inside and to develop their own sensational style!

AWARDS:
Bernina
Machine Workmanship
1994

LAURA HEINE

ONE FISH, TWO FISH, RED FISH, BLUE FISH
82" x 92", Laura Heine, Billings, MT, 1993. Cottons; machine pieced and machine quilted.
1996.01.21

MARILYN HENRION

I use color, line, and form much as a poet employs words to convey a particular emotion or idea.

As in poetry, the metaphorical images are meant to resonate, being both themselves and something they may suggest to the viewer. The works transcend the impersonal objectivity of geometric abstraction through the sensuousness of materials of which they are constructed, revealing a blend of reason and passion.

Paying homage to traditional techniques of hand piecing and hand quilting, my goal is to transform these materials into expressive works of art.

HERE BETWEEN
40.5" x 40.5", Marilyn Henrion, New York, NY, 1992. Cottons; machine pieced and hand quilted.
1997.07.12

*E*xperience judging at all levels, writing, teaching, and completing antique tops and blocks provide inspiration for Becky's own quiltmaking.

INDIAN BARN RAISING

86" x 96", Becky Herdle, Rochester, NY, 1988. Cottons; machine pieced and hand quilted.
2001.14.01

BECKY HERDLE

ETHEL HICKMAN

Like so many quilters, Ethel's involvement in quilting has been in phases and has been influenced by the work of others as well as her own innate sense of color and style.

ANN ORR'S "YE OLDE SAMPLER"

80" x 100", Ethel Hickman, Camden, AR, 1985. Poly/cotton blends, cottons; hand appliquéd, hand quilted with corded edge. 1997.06.02

A deep appreciation for beauty and workmanship guides Chizuko's quiltmaking.

GREAT AMERICAN ELK
65" x 70", Chizuko Hana Hill, Garland, TX, 1994. Cottons; machine and hand pieced, hand quilted.
1998.05.01

CHIZUKO HANA HILL

MARY KAY HITCHNER

I push myself to develop or learn something new with every quilt.

TULIPS AGLOW
54.5" x 54.5", Mary Kay Hitchner, Haverford, PA, 1989. Cottons; machine pieced and hand quilted.
1996.01.28

My quilts are a culmination of a lifelong exposure [to quilts] and sewing, and my love of history and need to create. Old textiles from all over the world are an endless source of inspiration and wonder.

Art school skills and years of experience with the sewing machine allow me to design and produce quilts that satisfy my desire to pay tribute to textile creators of the past.

Pat Holly

My personal goal in quilting is to continue to make machine-made quilts that are inspired by the traditions in quilting.

Traveling and teaching inspire my quilts, too.

I want to push myself to be as creative as possible and use the sewing machine to create my work.

Sue Nickels

Pat HOLLY & NICKELS Sue

THE BEATLES QUILT

95" x 95", Pat Holly, Muskegon, MI, and Sue Nickels, Ann Arbor, MI, 1998. Cottons; machine appliquéd, machine pieced, and machine quilted.
1998.01.01

AWARDS:

AQS

Best of Show

1998

Pat HOLLY & NICKELS Sue

THE SPACE QUILT

87" x 87", Sue Nickels, Ann Arbor, MI, and Pat Holly, Muskegon, MI, 2004. Cottons; polyester and metallic threads; machine pieced, machine appliquéd, and machine quilted. 2004.01.02

AWARDS:
Bernina
Machine Workmanship
2004

For me, quiltmaking is a perfect blending of the old and the new. I like to create fresh designs, then make the quilt the old-fashioned way—by hand.

With each quilt I hope to craft a piece that is visually appealing and constructed with top quality workmanship. Since I quilt purely for my own enjoyment, as long as I am pleased with the finished piece, then I have achieved my goal.

FEATHERED BEAUTIES
70" x 83", Pamela Humphries, Carriere, MI, 2005. Cottons, cotton and silk threads; hand pieced, appliquéd, and quilted. 2006.04.01

AWARDS:
AQS
Hand Workmanship
2006

MARION HUYCK

*L*etting the fabric speak and using it in new ways are at the core of Marion's quiltmaking.

TERRARIUM

40" x 50.5", Marion Huyck, Chicago, IL, 1983. Cottons; hand pieced, machine pieced, hand appliquéd, reverse appliquéd, and hand quilted and embroidered. 1997.06.82

AWARDS:

First Place – Wall Quilt, Professional

1986

NOTHING GOLD CAN STAY
71" x 57", Marion Huyck, Chicago, IL, 1985. Cottons; hand
pieced, machine pieced, hand appliquéd, reverse appliquéd, and
hand quilted.
1997.06.48

LOIS K. IDE

My mother taught me to sew on an old treadle Singer when I was only four years old. I am now 88 years old, still sewing and quilting, writing, and teaching occasionally. Mama also taught me to share my talents.

What could be more rewarding than designing and making and being asked to share my quilts in churches, at school, and in other meetings as well as in quilt shows?

Now I am making numerous crazy quilts from all the bushels of scraps I have saved through the years.

GALAXY OF QUILTERS

87" x 107", Lois K. Ide, Bucyrus, OH, 1983. Cottons and cotton blends; hand appliquéd, hand embroidered, machine pieced, and hand quilted.
1997.06.25

96

Although she only creates quilts of her own design, Katherine believes that the efforts of other quilt artists should be appreciated.

ORIENTAL FANTASY
82" x 98", Katherine Inman, Athens, OH, 1984. Cottons; machine pieced, hand appliquéd, hand embroidered, and hand quilted. 1996.01.22

AWARDS:
AQS
Best of Show
1985

KATHERINE INMAN

MICHAEL JAMES

ALETSCH

81" x 41", Michael James, Lincoln, NE, 1990. Cottons, silk; machine pieced and
machine quilted.
1997.06.01

One of my objectives is to challenge the notion of what quilts can be.

I want my imagery to point the viewer toward a deeper kind of looking, to provoke reflection, and perhaps to break down presumptions about what art is for.

Creating quilts for their families gave sisters-in-law Carolyn and Wilma the opportunity to produce and sell art of their own design. FEATHERED FRIENDS was the first quilt acquired in the collection.

FEATHERED FRIENDS
63" x 91", Carolyn Johnson and Wilma Johnson, Symsonia, KY, 1984. Cottons; hand appliquéd and hand quilted.
1997.06.20

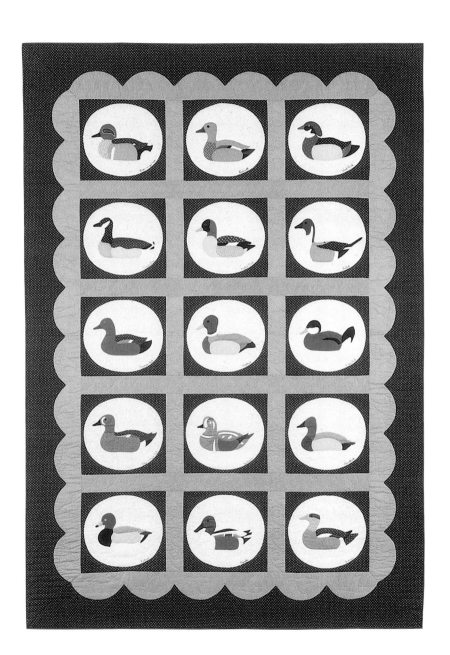

Carolyn
JOHNSON &

Wilma
JOHNSON

MELODY JOHNSON

HOT FUN
56" x 63," Melody Johnson, Cary, IL, 1995. Hand-dyed cottons; machine embroidered, fused, and machine quilted.
1996.01.14

Quiltmaking should be fun; if it isn't, why do it?

I'm not out to prove I can achieve some sort of perfection. I want to have a great time making a quilt and have it look like fun when it is finished.

I believe that the design is paramount to the technique, and whatever it takes to create that piece is the right way to do it. I'm making art for the wall, not a functional bed quilt.

I choose to fuse so I can be expressive with fabric in ways that would be impossible with any other construction method. Scissors are a drawing tool; unfinished edges add character.

I especially enjoy improvising, but often find myself making up a design found in my sketchbook.

AWARDS:
RJR
Best Wall Quilt
1995

Collection of The National Quilt Museum

My intent is to create something of beauty.

Using the California coastal area and other sites I experience as inspiration, my quilts reflect a love of nature. In combining painting with fabric techniques, I am working toward a rich surface. The texture of the commercial fabrics enhances the colors and painterly textures of the painting.

Adding quilting gives the work a relief structure with line work, like drawing over the color. The play of the quilting lines against both the piecing and painting adds an exciting visual element and suggests other layers of meaning. It also adds depth, like a relief sculpture.

If the viewer looks deeper than the surface richness, the elements used can be interpreted with symbology from several cultures that revere nature.

NIGHT BEACONS III

48" x 67", Vicki L. Johnson, Soquel, CA, 1991. Cottons; painted and machine appliquéd, machine and hand quilted.
1992.12.01

VICKI L. JOHNSON

ANGELA W. KAMEN

The confluence of geometry, fabrics, and original design are at the core of Angela's artistic expression through quilts.

JELLY BEAN

57" x 77", Angela W. Kamen, Bedford Corners, NY, 1998. Cottons and silk organza; machine pieced, machine quilted, machine embroidered and couched. 1998.02.01

AWARDS:
RJR
Best Wall Quilt
1998

A love of hand quilting sustained Margie's interest in quiltmaking throughout her lifetime.

CHERRY ROSE
95" x 94", Margie T. Karavitis, Spokane, WA, 1990. Cottons; hand appliquéd, hand and machine pieced, and hand quilted. 1992.13.01

MARGIE T. KARAVITIS

OH MY STARS
97" x 97", Margie T. Karavitis,
Spokane, WA, 1989. Cottons; hand
and machine pieced and hand quilted.
1992.15.01

AWARDS:
*First Place
Traditional Pieced,
Professional*
1990

Collection of The National Quilt Museum

I set personal goals for myself that keep stretching me beyond what I've done in the past.

I always keep open to new insights as I work and ask myself, "what if."

I don't very often have my quilts planned from start to finish. Many times I end up interjecting elements found around me in nature. I love to put little animals, birds, or insects on my quilts.

Ultimately, I quilt to please myself. I love owning beautiful, well-made things.

AWARDS:
AQS Hand Workmanship
2007

BONNIE KELLER

ORGANIC GARDEN

86.5" 86.5", Bonnie Keller, Chehalis, WA, 2006. Cottons, silk and cotton threads, Ultrasuede® embroidery floss, Pigma® pens, acrylic yarn, Tsukineko® all-purpose ink; hand appliquéd, machine pieced, hand quilted.
2007.08.01

SHIRLEY P. KELLY

FLOWERS OF THE CROWN
78.5" x 58", Shirley P. Kelly, Colden,
NY, 2002. Cottons, lamé, cotton and
rayon threads; hand appliquéd, machine
quilted.
2007.10.01

As an art student, I was encouraged to depict two-dimensional objects in an abstract or non-representational manner. But I always liked the challenge of realism, especially the unique utilitarian forms and shapes of animals.

My first time at an AQS show, the realistic depictions in the pictorial quilt categories inspired me to develop a prepared-edge applique technique, which I have used now for about twenty years.

The personalities of the animals or birds that inhabit my quilts appeal to children and adults alike. Over and over again they tell me that these quilts make them smile. That is the ultimate justification for my work.

AWARDS:
First Place
Pictorial Wall Quilt
2003

106

PANDAS 'ROUND THE WORLD
75" x 99", Shirley P. Kelly, Colden, NY,
1993. Cottons; hand appliquéd, machine
pieced, and machine quilted.
1997.07.14

AWARDS:
*Second Place
Amateur, Appliqué*
1994

SHIRLEY P. KELLY

SHRILEY P. KELLY

PUFFINS

78" x 71", Shirley P. Kelly, Colden, NY, 2004. Cottons; hand appliquéd, machine quilted.

2005.01.02

AWARDS:

Bernina

Machine Workmanship

2005

Collection of The National Quilt Museum

My quilts take their inspiration from old tile patterns and illuminated manuscripts.

I use interlace patterns to explore the intricacies of geometry.

In my work, hard-edged patterns contrast with the fluid qualities of nature.

MALTESE CROSS
76" x 88", Chris Kleppe, Milwaukee, WI, 1987. Cottons; hand and machine pieced and hand quilted.
1997.06.35

CHRIS KLEPPE

THERESA KLOSTERMAN

Filling time with beauty and practicality is the essence of Theresa's quilting efforts.

FLOWER BASKET SAMPLER

90" x 112", Theresa Klosterman, Mooreton, ND, 1984. Cottons and cotton blends; hand and machine pieced, hand quilted, and hand embroidered.
1997.06.23

SATURN'S RINGS

61" x 41", Susan Knight, Bay Village, OH, 1986. Cottons and linen; hand pieced, hand appliquéd, and hand quilted. 1997.06.68

*S*usan enjoys sharing the utility and creativity of quiltmaking with others.

MARZENNA J. KROL

Having learned to quilt from Mennonites in the Lancaster, Pennsylvania, area, Marzenna gained her understanding of and appreciation for quiltmaking's artistry through their patience and love for the art.

BASKET OF FLOWERS

72" x 82", Marzenna J. Krol, Carmel Valley, CA, 1982. Cottons/polyesters; hand appliquéd and hand quilted.
1997.06.03

MAPLE LEAF
84" x 97", Marzenna J. Krol, Carmel
Valley, CA, 1984. Cottons/polyesters;
hand appliquéd and hand quilted,
machine pieced.
1997.06.37

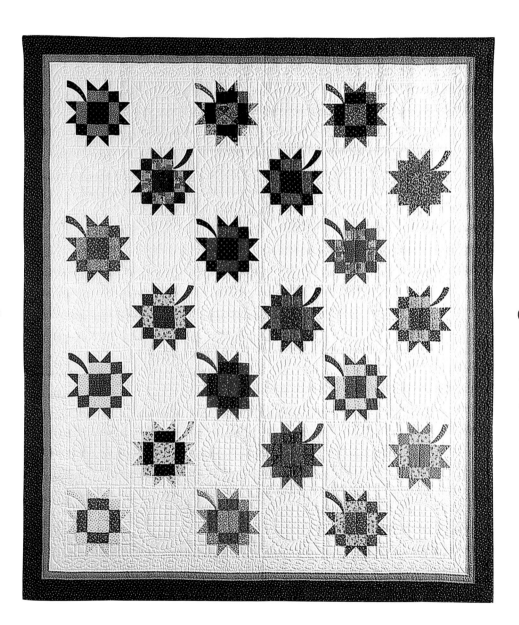

MARZENNA J. KROL

TONI KRON

To ensure that each quilt she designs remains one-of-a-kind, Toni destroys the pattern once the project is complete to preserve its artistic integrity.

ORCHARD BEAUTY
88" x 105", Toni Kron, Guntersville, AL, 1986. Cottons, dacron/cotton blends; hand appliquéd, quilted, and embroidered. 1997.06.50

*Q*uilting for Mary is not so much about achievement as it is a lifelong love of accomplishing beautiful, handmade items.

MANY STAR
77" x 96", Mary E. Kuebler, Cincinnati, OH, 1984. Cottons; batiked and hand quilted.
1997.06.36

JAN LANAHAN

Quilting is but one entryway into the universe of textile artistry for Jan.

BASKETS AND THE CORN
67" x 80", Jan Lanahan, Walkersville, MD, 1986. Cottons and linens; embroidered, hand painted, machine pieced, and hand quilted.
1992.07.01

AWARDS:
First Place
Theme: Baskets
1988

REACH FOR THE STARS
66" x 82", Jan Lanahan, Walkersville, MD,
1986. Cottons, flannels, satins; hand pieced
and hand quilted.
1997.06.61

AWARDS:
Second Place
Innovative Pieced, Amateur
1987

JAN LANAHAN

JUDITH LARZELERE

RED SQUARED

59" x 59", Judith Larzelere, Westerly, RI, 1992. Cottons; machine pieced and quilted.
2008.01.01

I work abstractly and I am interested in setting up an ambiguous figure/ground dialogue through the manipulation of hue and value.

I feel committed to piecing because I see it as the most unique aspect of art making in this medium.

Form follows from the way that my quilts are made. Strip-piecing generates a non-pictorial, linear, abstract, non-geometric image by its process.

Piecing is what sets quilters apart from all other art media and allows us to generate images that no one else in their right mind would attempt.

To gain an individual artist's signature style is the goal of any professional; piecing gives those who rely on it a private aesthetic world to explore. For this reason I champion cutting and sewing.

We all want to be remembered by our families, by descendents as yet unknown, and by our quilt communities. Our work is evidence of how we choose to be remembered.

The ties may be artistic or literary, profound or humorous, functional or aesthetic, but we want to leave something of ourselves.

My own work indicates a very personal perspective and expresses my need to see us laugh and to leave the world a more peaceful, exciting, and caring place in which to live.

LISTEN TO YOUR MOTHER
43" x 43", Jean Ray Laury, Clovis, CA, 1997. Cottons; hand screen printed and machine quilted.
2001.04.01

LIBBY LEHMAN

ESCAPADE
80" x 80", Libby Lehman, Houston, TX, 1993. Cottons; rayon and metallic thread; machine pieced, machine embroidered, and machine quilted.
1997.07.09

When I make a quilt, it is first and foremost to please me. If I'm not happy with it, how can I expect anyone else to be? It is icing on the cake when others like my work, especially if they like it enough to buy it!

I would love for my quilts to be seen and admired for years to come. I try to use quality products and excellent workmanship. However, I won't be around to know what will happen years from today.

It gives me great pleasure to see my quilts hanging at The National Quilt Museum in the company of so many brilliant works of art. I know that ESCAPADE and STAR-CROSSED are in the hands of experts who will take great care of them. Thanks, guys

AWARDS:
First Place
Other Techniques
1993

STAR-CROSSED
70" x 70", Libby Lehman, Houston, TX, 1986. Cottons and cotton blends; machine pieced and hand quilted. 1997.06.76

LIBBY LEHMAN

MYRL LEHMAN-TAPUNGOT

I have always had an over-active imagination, and early on realized that I would never have enough time in one lifetime to see all of the designs I dreamed up completed.

In 1979 after my husband retired from the US Navy, we retired to the island of Mindanao in the Philippines. Mindanaoans are very clever and talented, and in the years since our arrival we have been able to train over 400 people in making some of the most beautiful quilts imaginable.

LE JARDIN DE NOS REVES (MY GARDEN OF DREAMS)

68" x 88", Myrl Lehman-Tapungot, Cagayan de Oro, Philippines, 1997. Cottons; hand quilted with trapunto and hand embroidered and beaded. MAQS 1997.01.01

AWARDS:
Gingher
Hand Workmanship
2005

I am passionate about the traditional American quilt, and that unique style is always reflected in my designs.

I fell in love with the original, elegant applique quilts of the Baltimore Album period and the infamous Emporia, Kansas, era. These quilts have had a profound impact on me and my approach to quilts and their design, as well as defining for me true artistry and craftsmanship when applied to the traditional art of quiltmaking.

My goal has always been to design and create one-of-a-kind hand appliqué quilts with careful attention to detail and workmanship. I like the test of translating the designs I see in my head into quilts that use challenging traditional quilt techniques to achieve a fresh updated look.

AWARDS:
RJR
Best Wall Quilt
2005

Collection of The National Quilt Museum

SANDRA LEICHNER

UNEXPECTED BEAUTY

51" x 67", Sandra Leichner, Albany, OR, 2004, Cottons; cotton, silk, and polyester threads; fabric paint, rock crystals, wool batting; hand and machine pieced; hand appliquéd, embroidered, and beaded; machine quilted.
2005.01.03

LILLIAN J. LEONARD

*C*ompetition is its own reward as Lillian creates quilts for contests.

TRANQUILITY
98" x 92", Lillian J. Leonard, Indianapolis, IN, 1985. Cottons; hand pieced, hand appliquéd, and hand quilted. 1997.06.85

TRANQUILITY (wallhanging)
34" x 34", Lillian J. Leonard, Indianapolis,
IN, 1985.
1997.06.84

LILLIAN J. LEONARD

BARKING UP THE WRONG TREE

58" x 45", Sharon Malec, West Chicago, IL, 1999. Cottons and cotton blends; hand painted, machine appliquéd, machine couched, and machine quilted.
2000.04.01

AWARDS:
Third Place
Theme Wall: Dogwoods
2000

*A*s a quilt artist, I have a love of fabrics. It is a wonderfully colorful and tactile medium, resulting in art work with a soft expression. I am particularly drawn to nature's colors which complement the animal and nature themes that dominate my work. A variety of hand and machine techniques are used to create my quilts.

126

Collection of The National Quilt Museum

DESERT DUSK

53" x 43", Marguerite Ann Malwitz, Brookfield, CT, 1988. Cottons, blends, silks, and satins; cotton and metallic threads; tie-dyed, machine and hand pieced, hand quilted. 1997.07.06

Sharing her life's journey as a Christian artist is the focus of Marguerite's studio art quiltmaking.

Inge
MARDAL &
Steen
HOUGS

IT'S NOT SUMMER YET

54" x 41", Inge Mardal, Brussels, Belgium, 2000. Cottons; hand appliquéd, machine embroidered, and machine quilted.
2001.13.01

AWARDS:

RJR

Best Wall Quilt

2001

The way we work makes each quilt a part of a continuum, building on previous experience and guided by new ideas for realization of the next piece.

We process intellectually and artistically what we see of interest and are open for new inspiration. We consequently do not have preconceived ideas on which directions to follow in terms of motifs, styles, or techniques.

It will be very exciting to see to where that will be leading us.

SUN-BATHING BLUE TIT
66" x 80", Inge Mardal, Chantilly, France,
2003. Cottons; hand painted and machine
quilted.
2004.01.03

AWARDS:
RJR
Best Wall Quilt
2004

Inge
MARDAL & Steen HOUGS

SUZANNE MARSHALL

An image from the past, thumbing through a library book, or walking down the street of a foreign city may plant a seed in my mind that may inspire a quilt.

Starting with this small inspiration, a quilt may begin without my knowing how it will evolve.

As I work, the quilt itself helps me know what to do next.

The finished quilt is always a surprise, often surpassing any initial concept.

AWARDS:
*Timeless Treasures
Hand Workmanship*
2002

MOTHER'S DAY

81" x 81", Suzanne Marshall, Clayton, MO, 2001. Cottons; hand appliquéd, hand embroidered, and hand quilted.
2002.01.01

TOUJOURS NOUVEAU
69" x 80", Suzanne Marshall, Clayton, MO, 1993. Cottons; hand appliquéd with embroidery and hand quilted. Named one of the 100 Best American Quilts of the 20th Century.
1996.01.27

AWARDS:
Gingher
Hand Workmanship
1993

SUZANNE MARSHALL

KATIE PASQUINI MASOPUST

I hope to create beautiful, thought-provoking art quilts for the viewers, but mainly I make them because that is how I express my creative energies.

I love working on every aspect of the quiltmaking process.

Making art quilts makes me happy.

TENERAMENTE
(WITH TENDER EMOTION)

50" x 63", Katie Pasquini Masopust, Santa Fe, NM, 2006. Cottons, satin, Ultrasuede; transparent, cotton, and polyester threads; wool batting. Machine appliquéd and quilted.

2007.03.01

Collection of The National Quilt Museum

Intricacy of design and workmanship excellence guide Noriko's artistry, which is inspired by daily life as well as spiritual interests.

AWARDS:
First Place
Mixed Techniques
1997

NORIKO MASUI

A MANDALA OF FLOWERS

76" x 81", Noriko Masui, Saitama, Japan, 1997. Cottons, silks, polyesters, and materials from Japanese kimonos and obis; hand pieced, hand appliquéd, and hand quilted.
1998.04.01

JEAN K. MATHEWS

PERSIAN PARADISE
59" x 72.5", Jean K. Mathews, Marco Island, FL, 1986. Cottons and polyester/cotton chintz; hand appliquéd, reverse appliquéd, and hand quilted.
1997.06.55

In thinking about what I hope to achieve in quiltmaking, I must reflect on the 28 years since I began making quilts.

It is amazing to think back to cutting with templates only, hand piecing and quilting, and uninspiring fabrics. Today we have wonderful rotary cutters, ¼" presser feet, the artistry of free-motion quilting, and best of all, the beautiful fabrics, great magazines, shops, and fantastic shows to inspire us.

Being fulfilled with pushing my creativity to new limits, the satisfaction of having my work in shows, and helping others to learn, along with the gratitude and praise my family bestows on me every time I make a quilt for them, has been wonderful. I hope I am given good health to achieve more of the same.

Total immersion in every aspect of quilting, from collecting to production to appreciation of others' work, informs Laverne's approach to quiltmaking.

STRAWBERRY SUNDAE
64" x 83", Laverne N. Mathews, Orange, TX, 1986. Cottons and cotton blends; hand appliquéd and hand quilted. 1997.06.78

AWARDS:
Second Place
Appliqué, Amateur
1987

LAVERNE N. MATHEWS

LAVERNE MATHEWS

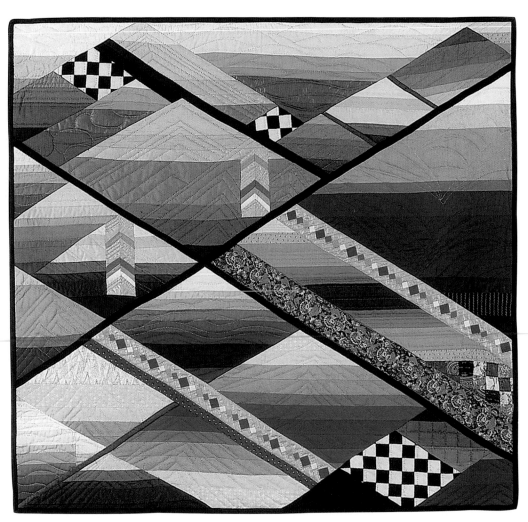

TAOS TAPESTRY

37" x 40", Laverne Mathews, Orange, TX, 1986. Cottons and cotton blends; machine pieced and hand quilted.
1997.06.81

Quilt making has been very rewarding for me, creatively and professionally.

I enjoy the process and the result. I hope that others enjoy my quilts, but I make them for myself.

Being able to teach quilt making has allowed me to travel far beyond my expectations and to meet wonderful people.

NEW DIRECTIONS
76" x 92", Judy Mathieson, Sebastopol, CA, 1996. Cottons; machine pieced, and hand and machine quilted.
2001.07.01

JUDY MATHIESON

KARIN MATTHIESEN

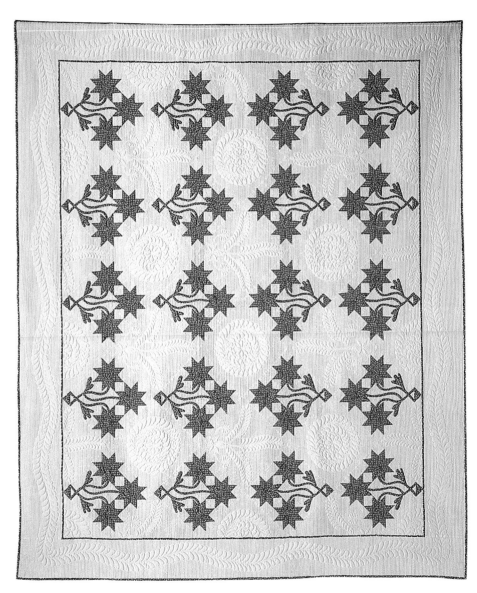

Appliqué was her initial inspiration to start quilting; a desire to achieve excellent workmanship and try new styles and techniques guides Karin's current efforts.

BED OF PEONIES
85" x 96", Karin Matthiesen, Madison, WI, 1986. Cottons; hand appliquéd and hand quilted.
1996.01.04

AWARDS:
Gingher
Hand Workmanship
1986

First Place
Traditional Patchwork,
Professional
1986

Collection of The National Quilt Museum

Achievement is a combination of effort, learning new skills, and artistry.

STARRY, STARRY NIGHT
75" x 90", Mary Jo McCabe, Davenport, IA, 1985. Cottons; hand pieced and hand quilted.
1997.06.77

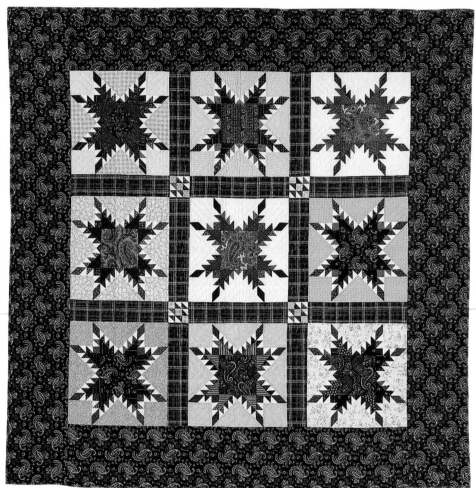

MARSHA McCLOSKEY

True artistry in one's craft is achievement at the highest level.

STAR OF CHAMBLIE
67" x 67", Marsha McCloskey, Seattle, WA, 1986. Cottons; machine pieced and hand quilted.
2001.05.01

Like an artist in any medium, I make my artwork because it is personally exhilarating to do.

My quilts express who I am and what interests me. They communicate that excitement and personal expression to many other people.

The process of working in this medium is endlessly fascinating. It's a journey with many passages, interweavings, forks in the road, and an unknown ending.

The tactile quality of fibers, the endlessly varied patterns and glorious subtleties of color, the physical movements involved in cutting and sewing—all are unique to the medium. The association of the fabrics to other lives and places is a source of contemplation.

Creation, exhilaration, self-expression, communication, tactile pleasure, visual treats, meditation, and contemplation are achievements that very few careers produce.

RUTH McDOWELL

NA PALI

70" x 77", Ruth McDowell, Winchester, MA, 1999. Cottons; machine pieced, hand-appliquéd boat, and machine quilted.
2001.06.01

KEIKO MIYAUCHI

I have loved floral quilts ever since seeing the Whitehill Collection quilts at the Denver Museum in 1986. I've made floral quilts ever since.

Roses, cosmos, Gerbera daisies, and lilies, along with animals, populate my quilts. I try to sew with passion and precision.

I hope my quilts speak to the need to care for our planet's flowers and animals.

Hopefully my quilts make people happy, stay in their minds, and encourage them to become quiltmakers, too.

AWARDS:
Timeless Treasures
Hand Workmanship
2001

BLUE EARTH FILLED WITH WATER AND FLOWERS
76" x 83", Keiko Miyauchi, Nagano, Japan, 2000. Hand-dyed cottons, polyester; hand appliquéd, trapuntoed, and hand quilted.
2001.12.01

Family quilts nurtured my early love of quilts. They were windows into the lives of my mother's family and perpetuated this wonderful tradition.

Quilts speak volumes about their makers' lives, as my quilts have been reflective of 36 years of my life changes.

Through designs, fabrics, and colors, my enthusiasm and encouragement for all quilters and their talents remain constant.

With my quilts—created for physical and emotional warmth, for self, gift, or purchase—the teaching of techniques, the enjoyment of the sewing process, and the promotion of bonds between quilters are the most important elements of my quiltmaking.

MARY GOLDEN MOODY

NE'ER ENCOUNTER PAIN
90" x 90", Mary Golden, Gloucester, MA, 1982. Cottons; hand pieced and hand quilted.
1997.06.42

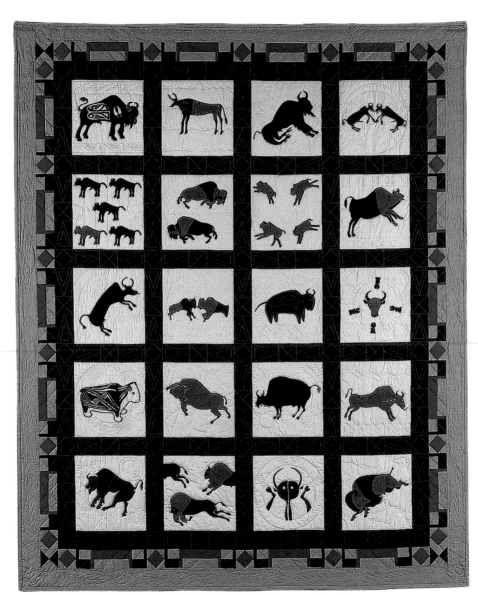

Barbara Pettinga MOORE

Combining a love for and background in art and science, especially wildlife, lies at the heart of Barbara's approach to quiltmaking and other artistic endeavors.

BUFFALO MAGIC
75" x 90", Barbara Pettinga Moore, Shelburne, VT, 1984. Cotton/poly blend, suede cloth; hand appliquéd and hand quilted.
1997.06.09

AWARDS:
First Quilt
1986

Collection of The National Quilt Museum

Carole Adams
Mona Barker
Linda Cantrell
Rhoda Cohen
Shannie J. Coyne
Pat Cox
Barbara Crane
Joe Cunningham
Ronnie Durrance
Elly Dyson
Chris Wolf Edmonds
Victoria Faoro
Lee Farrington
Cathy Grafton
Roberta Horton
Lois K. Ide
Jean Johnson
Ed Larson (with Sarah Hass)
Masami Kato
Helen Kelly
Donna Makim
Gwen Marston
Judy Mathieson
Carolyn Muller
Paula Nadelstern
Dawn Rappold
Art Salemme
Steve Schutt
Joan Schulze
Elaine Sparlin
Susan Turbak
Emma Martin Yost

Artists from THE PROGRESSIVE
PICTORIAL QUILT
Caron L. Mosey, coordinator

THE PROGRESSIVE PICTORIAL QUILT

44" x 44", artists in *America's Pictorial Quilts*, coordinated by Caron L. Mosey, 1987. Cottons and cotton blends; hand appliquéd, embroidered, and quilted; machine pieced.
1991.01.01

MARY MORGAN

Being a self-taught quilter has given Mary deep respect for quilters who made beautiful quilts without formal art training or unlimited, inspirational supplies. She is more concerned with what her quilts do than what they say.

DIFFRACTIONS III
65" x 94", Mary Morgan, Little Rock, AR, 1989. Hand-dyed cottons; machine pieced and hand quilted.
1997.06.16

My artistic aspirations can be described as similar to the *Star Trek* mission: "Boldly going where no one has gone before."

It is the process of experimentation and the joy of discovery that excites me.

The work of my hands is essential to my well-being, with the objective always to make something that is unique and beautiful.

I use my curiosity and creativity to seek new possibilities in my ongoing adventures with textile art.

AWARDS:
RJR
Best Wall Quilt
1997

LAURA MURRAY

HELIACAL RISE
71" x 74", Laura Murray, Minneapolis, MN, 1996. Cottons and silks; hand painted, hand and machine pieced, and machine quilted.
1997.03.01

JOYCE MURRIN

BEACH ROSES
79" x 49", Joyce Murrin, Orient, NY, 1986.
Cottons and cotton blends, some hand dyed;
machine pieced and hand quilted.
1997.06.05

My greatest joy in quiltmaking is the challenge—met head on and accomplished.

Whether it's refusing to compensate a line in the design or fighting my self to keep a color or particular fabric in the process and maybe losing in the end, it's all worth the challenge!

My desire to design pieced quilts with many non-traditional angles has been my most rewarding challenge. I met that technical challenge by working until I perfected setting in any angle, using any fabric, easily.

Now I have the freedom to be creative, to think and design artistically, and in the end, to make quilts from my own designs that are complex yet visually uncomplicated; still challenging; sometimes surprising; and for many reasons, pleasing to me.

The quilts that I make are always the culmination of much agonizing and mind-changing.

There never seems to be a straight path from first idea to last stitch.

I want my quilts to be objects of curiosity to the viewer, not just one-glance wonders. My hope is that the viewer will be intrigued and spend some time looking at my quilts, puzzling over how I did that, or WHY I did that.

I also would like to inspire viewers to try something different—to carry away some small seed that will blossom into a new direction for their own work. That's what I hope to achieve!

AWARDS:
RJR
Best Wall Quilt
2002

CLAUDIA CLARK MYERS

WHO'S YOUR POPPY?
61" x 62", Claudia Clark Myers, Duluth, MN, 2001. Cottons; machine paper pieced, machine appliquéd, machine embroidered, and machine quilted.
2002.02.01

JAN MYERS-NEWBURY

Known for her work with geometrics and shibori dyeing techniques, Jan's art is also informed by pattern.

PRECIPICE
75" x 93", Jan Myers-Newbury, Pittsburgh, PA, 1989. Hand dyed cottons; machine pieced and machine quilted.
2001.08.01

I make quilts because I love to sew and quilting satisfies my creative needs!

I want to draw the viewer in with a large dramatic design. Then I want them to come close, study the detail, and understand how much pleasure I get from making a quilt, maybe inspire them to have a go at stitching any way they want.

If the viewer is never going to sew, I'd like them to go away from my quilt feeling that their day is brighter and better because of what they have just seen.

My aims are to continue to explore and develop my work, to improve, to keep enjoying it all (even the boring repetitive bits!), and to continue to share what I do with others.

AWARDS:
Hancock's of Paducah
Best of Show
2003

PHILIPPA NAYLOR

LIME LIGHT
81" x 81," Philippa Naylor, Dhahran, Saudi Arabia, 2002. Hand-dyed and painted cottons; machine pieced, trapuntoed, and machine quilted.
2003.01.01

PHILIPPA NAYLOR

POP STARS
86" x 86," Philippa Naylor, Dhahran,
Saudi Arabia, 2002. Hand-dyed cottons; machine pieced, trapuntoed, and
machine quilted.
2002.03.01

AWARDS:
Bernina
Machine Workmanship
2002

Before she passed away, Julia reflected that quiltmaking was only a hobby for her. The only quilt she did not keep is the one in the collection.

TENNESSEE PINK MARBLE
72" x 88", Julia Overton Needham, Knoxville, TN, 1991. Cottons, cotton blends; hand pieced, appliquéd, and quilted. 1996.01.26

AWARDS:
Gingher
Hand Workmanship
1991

JULIA OVERTON NEEDHAM

BARBARA NEWMAN

STARDUST
88" x 88", Barbara Newman, Brandon, MS, 2007. Cottons; hand pieced, appliquéd, and quilted.
2008.04.01

My love for the art of quilt-making began in 1991. As I made my first quilt, I knew I had found my creative inspiration.

From that day forward my hope was to create handmade quilts that would continue the tradition of our mothers and grandmothers. I strive to achieve the ability to make quilts of my own design and my version of antique quilts that have inspired me.

What I hope to achieve through the artistry of quilt-making is to inspire those quilters who view my work to experience the joy of creating quilts by hand, and to leave a legacy to my children and grandchildren that they can hold and know that my love for them was stitched into each quilt.

AWARDS:
AQS
Hand Workmanship
2008

Hallie's artistry is a combination of using hand-dyed fabric, silk screening some fabrics, judicious use of photographs, and intricate hand-stitched quilting.

ZINNIAS IN THE WINDOWS OF MY LOG CABIN
77" x 85", Hallie H. O'Kelley, Tuscaloosa, AL, 1987. Cottons; machine pieced and hand quilted.
1997.06.34

AWARDS:
Second Place
Theme: Log Cabin
1987

ANNE J. OLIVER

MOMMA'S GARDEN
88" x 91", Anne J. Oliver, Alexandria, VA, 1992. Cottons; hand appliquéd and hand quilted.
1996.01.19

*I*t was my fervent desire to reach the frustrated quilter who just might find ways to get over quilting hurdles by using freezer paper in the creation of quality quilts. All of my work has been done with the aid of freezer paper. More often than not, freezer paper took me over rough spots without losing that quality.

I firmly believe I would not have created award-winning quilts if I had not taken freezer paper out of the kitchen and put it into the sewing room. It helped me to compete with the "Big Boys." It made me more creative, gave me lots of fun, eliminated my frustrations, and brought me new friends from many places. FREEZER PAPER, take a bow, you did good!

AWARDS:
AQS
Best of Show
1992

Collection of The National Quilt Museum

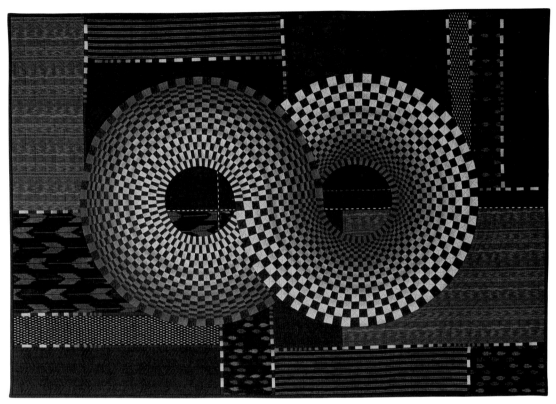

The entire process of creating a quilt is "sew" much fun:
- shopping—feeling and seeing the tempting colors and prints;
- viewing photos and paintings and imagining how they might translate into a quilt;
- traveling and composing photos to inspire future designs; and playing with color and textures while dyeing fabric.

Creating quilts allows me to use my favorite objects—needle, fabric, color, and thread—my senses, and my imagination.

I hope to touch the viewer with my vision: What does the viewer see from a distance and up close? How might the viewer use what I have done to create something new and original?

INFINITY

58" x 40", Nancy Ota, San Clemente, CA, 2005. Cottons, cotton/linen, yukata (cotton kimono) fabric; machine pieced, hand appliquéd, sashiko, machine quilted. 2006.06.01

AWARDS:
Moda
Best Wall Quilt
2006

Collection of The National Quilt Museum

BETTY K. PATTY

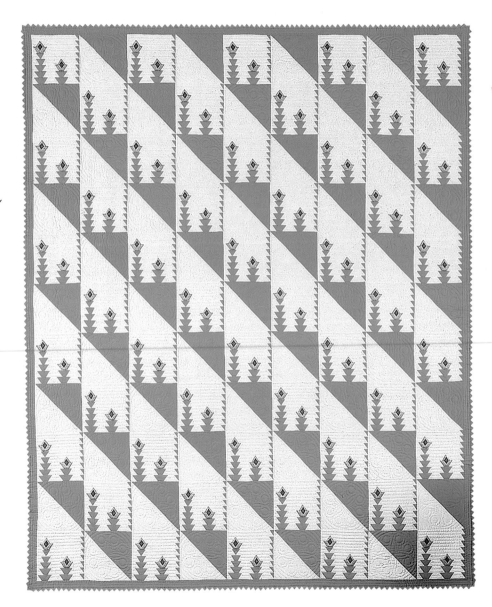

My interest in quilting has not lessened, although I lost my best friend and supporter, husband Dale, in 2003. It was good to have my quilting to fall back on.

I have slowed down creating full-sized hand quilted pieces and am making/donating crib quilts with three other members of our "Four Squares" group. The quilts are given to the Dayton (Ohio) Children's Hospital We have well surpassed the 1,000th quilt now and are still counting.

I did win some honors from the Ohio Bicentennial contest in 2003 with a quilt that is now in the Ohio Historical Museum.

I still tell my friends to enter the AQS Show at Paducah, as it is such an exciting contest to be involved with.

COUNTRY GARDEN
80" x 96", Betty K. Patty, Bradford, OH, 1985. Cottons; machine pieced, hand appliquéd, and hand quilted with trapunto. 1997.06.14

A love of history, including quilt history and placing current events into historical context, and devotion to family are the focus of Joyce's quiltmaking.

MOUNT ST. HELENS, DID YOU TREMBLE?

79" x 95", Joyce B. Peaden, Prosser, WA, 1991. Cottons, metallic fabrics; hand and machine appliquéd, machine pieced, Seminole pieced, and hand quilted. 1991.02.01

JOYCE B. PEADEN

SYLVIA PICKELL

ESCAPE FROM CIRCLE CITY

76" x 86", Sylvia Pickell, Sumter, SC, 1986. Cottons and polyblends; machine pieced, hand appliquéd, and hand quilted.
1997.06.19

I was born to stitch and to use my skills to educate others.

I learned techniques through classes or taught myself. I added my personal style and created award-winning quilts that I could share. I melded my education background and stitching skills and taught others. I achieved the designation of CJ, NQA in order to instruct in a different venue.

During an alternate career in financial management, volunteer hours have been spent exhibiting, teaching, and constructing at the local university, art gallery, and community theater; judging local quilt events; and sharing my collections and skills with interested groups.

I hope I have achieved inspiration, sparked creativity, encouraged, and educated with my art.

AWARDS:
First Place
Innovative Pieced, Amateur
1987

Collection of The National Quilt Museum

Paul Pilgrim's quilts reflect his many facets—complex, accomplished, fashionable, entertaining—and are as fresh today as when he made them.

He was about saving the efforts of others, no matter how humble. By incorporating pieces of unfinished projects from the past in his own work, he memorialized many anonymous quiltmakers.

Paul gave license to adopt, improve upon, and complete many unfinished projects that would have eventually been lost forever.

His energy is what is so apparent in his quilts and although he is no longer with us, his spirit, boundless enthusiasm, encouragement, and joy live on through his quilts. His work is still teaching, which, of course, was his passion along with collecting antique quilts.

Gerald Roy

PAUL D. PILGRIM

DRESDEN GARDEN

85" x 86", Paul D. Pilgrim, Oakland, CA, 1992; quilted by Toni Fisher, Belton, MO. Cottons and 1940s' Dresden Plate blocks; hand pieced, hand appliquéd, machine pieced, and hand quilted. 1997.05.17

My quilts are stories about events, actions, energy, place, past, and future. I invite people to question the thoughts that led to the design:

Appliqué quilts from the 1990s began as a puzzle—pieces fit together to create new design;

Titles spark interest—WAITING FOR PINK LINOLEUM, IT'S ALL IN THE TIMING, ANSWERING THE RIDDLE.

Quilts in 2000 are abstract—colors, shapes, memories as starting point:

RETURN TO SAN JUAN recalls an award-winning oil painting;

MONKEY SIGHTING color fields reflect quilts from the 1980s;

BLUEBIRDS FLY echoes sentiments from a past fiber art creation.

I ask the viewer to look at my art quilts from a distance to see color and enthusiasm. On closer view, luscious colors side by side create a bold design.

ON WEDNESDAY MORNING
50" x 70", Yvonne Porcella, Modesto, CA, 1995. Cottons; machine pieced, hand appliquéd and quilted
2001.10.01

Over 25 years ago I learned how to quilt from my grandmother. I find hand quilting relaxing because it gives me time to think and communicate with God. It is also rewarding to see the end results of transforming fabric into a beautiful work of art.

I hope to keep the heritage of quiltmaking alive so that the art of hand quilting will not be lost.

My quilts incorporate traditional techniques while at the same time combining my own contemporary touches. Each quilt truly has a personality of its own, whether it be whimsical, flamboyant, or serious.

As an artist, I hope to pass on the inspiration and knowledge about quiltmaking to start others on this wonderful journey.

AWARDS:
AQS
Best of Show
1994

WILD ROSE
90" x 90", Fay Pritts, Mt. Pleasant, PA, 1993. Cottons; hand appliquéd and hand quilted.
1996.01.30

FAY PRITTS

JULEE PROSE

The thrill of competition and an appreciation for fine detail and precision are at the heart of Julee's quiltmaking.

COMMUNITY BARN RAISING
78" x 105", Julee Prose, Ottumwa, IA, 1987. Cottons; hand appliquéd, machine pieced, and hand quilted. 1997.06.12

AWARDS:
First Place
Theme: Log Cabin
1987

Collection of The National Quilt Museum

The challenges involved in quilting are what spur Doris's creativity. Learning new techniques or having to improvise her way out of a technical problem give her the sense of achievement and satisfaction.

FEATHERED STAR BOUQUET
77" x 77", Doris Amiss Rabey, Hyattsville, MD, 1987. Cottons; hand quilted, pieced, and appliquéd.
1992.03.01

DORIS AMISS RABEY

DORIS AMISS RABEY

PRESIDENT'S WREATH VARIATION
72" x 96", Doris Amiss Rabey, Hyattsville, MD, 1986. Cottons and cotton/polyesters; hand appliquéd, machine pieced, and hand quilted.
1997.06.58

AWARDS:
Second Place
Appliqué, Amateur
1986

When I start a quilt, it is because I must explore an idea. I let it take me where it will.

Each quilt is an exciting discovery of possibilities for me—in other words, big girl's play!

AUTUMN RADIANCE
81" x 93", Sharon Rauba, Riverside, IL, 1986. Cottons and cotton blends; hand appliquéd, machine pieced, and hand quilted.
1996.01.03

AWARDS:
AQS
Best of Show
1987

SHARON RAUBA

WENDY M. RICHARDSON

Creating nurtures me and is made more special when it connects with the world around me.

It is a joy to celebrate color and pattern and texture, whether to convey a message or simply for the beauty of it.

When it speaks to others— that is the most important achievement of all.

BASKETS I
80" x 96", Wendy M. Richardson, Brooklyn Park, MN, 1984. Cottons; machine pieced, hand appliquéd, embroidered, and quilted.
1997.06.04

168

Approaching quilting from a painter's point of view allows Lucretia to merge her love of drawing and her passion for artistic expression in the medium of fabric.

CITYSCAPE
50" x 64", Lucretia Romey, East Orleans, MA,1984. Cottons, cottons blends, and metallic fabrics; hand pieced and hand quilted.
1997.06.10

AWARDS:
First Place
Wall Quilt, Professional
1985

LUCRETIA ROMEY

SOLVEIG RONNQVIST

DISTANT CLOSENESS

75" x 50", Solveig Ronnqvist, Exeter, RI, 1986. Cottons and satins; machine pieced, machine
appliquéd, hand appliquéd, and machine quilted.
1997.06.17

Original designs worked up in smaller quilts are Solveig's métier. Foundations of traditional Finnish needlework skills, a class with Jean Ray Laury, and a fashion design degree all reveal themselves in her quilts.

170

I am a fiber artist. With fabric and thread, design, color, texture, and form, I strive to tell stories about the possibility of beauty, encouraging the viewer to imagine something out of the realm of their own reality, thus allowing them the opportunity to dream about beautiful things.

Designing and creating fabric—and using those fabrics in my art quilts—is my passion, the thing I cannot possibly be happy without doing.

My art quilts usually involve a back-story, or an interpretation of legend, myth, or history. By allowing the story to become my momentary reality, my imagination takes me to another place, another time, another life.

My hope is that my fabrics and art quilts do that for the people who view them.

AWARDS:
RJR Best Wall Quilt
1999

LONNI ROSSI

CABINS IN THE COSMOS

50" x 55", Lonni Rossi, Wynnewood, PA, 1998. Commercial, hand-dyed, surface designed cottons; gold lamé, computer chips, aviation artifact; machine pieced, quilted, and stitched; and fused. 1999.03.01

ADRIEN ROTHSCHILD

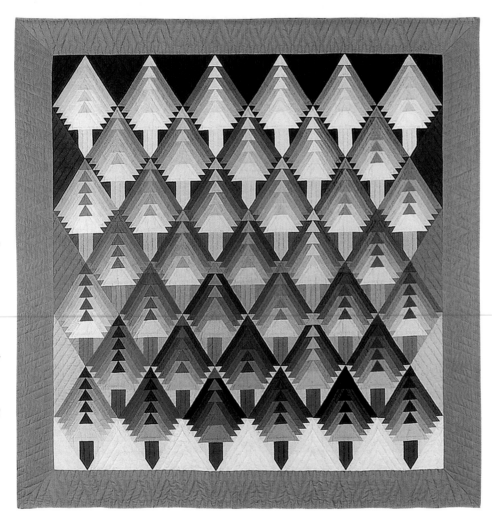

Art, mechanics, organics, and quilting professionally describe Adrien's achievements.

DESIGNER CHRISTMAS TREES
62" x 62", Adrien Rothschild, Baltimore, MD, 1990. Hand-dyed cottons; machine pieced and hand quilted.
1991.03.01

AWARDS:
Second Place
Wall Quilt, Amateur
1991

My quilts, like my paintings, are personal expressions I am compelled to create for my own well being. I am pleased when others can relate to them, but creating "ART" is the furthest thing from my mind. I am doing what I have to do and what I have been trained to do in order to satisfy and feel accomplished.

As we evolve so does the work. The joy is when someone else can relate to your experiences and react to the work because it triggers some personal response in them.

To respect and honor the inherent abilities of the medium and use it to its best advantage is the key.

GERALD E. ROY

COMPLIMENTARY COMPOSITION

64" x 65", Gerald Roy, Warner, NH, 1998/1999. Cottons; hand appliquéd, machine assembled, and hand quilted by Toni Fisher.
2004.04.01

LINDA M. ROY

SPICE OF LIFE
82" x 82", Linda M. Roy, Pittsfield, MA, 2003. Cottons; metallic thread and perle cotton embroidery; machine pieced, hand appliquéd and quilted.
2004.01.01

My joy in quiltmaking is to make something lasting that reflects my inner person.

My hopes are that my quilts bring the viewer a moment of reflection and feelings of peace and contentment, if only for a few minutes.

I consider most of my quilts "heirloom," and hope they are around for generations for my family to enjoy on a bed or on a wall.

I find it enjoyable savoring and not rushing the design or handwork, taking the time to find a way to get each design from my mind and sketched onto graph paper and then sewn into the fabrics.

My quilts are definitely not quickly made, and I hope they reflect the love and patience it took to complete each one.

AWARDS:
Hancock's of Paducah
Best of Show
2004

Collection of The National Quilt Museum

In her lifetime, Margaret went from making the utilitarian quilts of rural Kentucky to producing more contemporary work to sharing her skills and vision with young quilters.

SOPHISTICATION
55.5" x 55.5", Margaret Rudd, Cadiz, KY, 1987, designed by Ross Tucker, Corydon, IN. Cottons, silk, suede cloth; machine pieced and hand quilted.
1993.02.01

MARGARET RUDD

LINDA KAREL SAGE

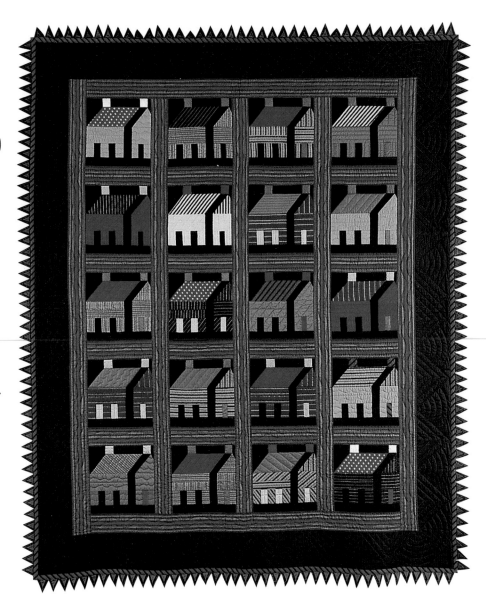

In my quiltmaking I hope to gladden the heart of the viewer with color, pattern, and texture.

I want my quilts to be fun for the viewer.

BROWN COUNTY LOG CABINS

87" x 93", Linda Karel Sage, Morgantown, IN, 1985. Cottons, cotton blends; machine pieced and hand quilted.
1997.06.08

AWARDS:
First Place
Traditional Patchwork, Amateur
1986

INDIANA CRAZY
70" x 71", Linda Karel Sage,
Morgantown, IN, 1988. Cottons
and blends; machine and hand
pieced; hand appliquéd, painted,
embroidered, tied, and quilted.
1997.06.30

LINDA KAREL SAGE

LYN PEARE SANDBERG

BOAT IN A BOTTLE SAMPLER

80" x 92", Lyn Peare Sandberg, Capitola, CA, 1988. Cottons; machine pieced and hand quilted.
1992.09.01

What I hope to achieve with my artistry is such a hard question for an artist, as artistry isn't that linear. What we achieve with it is in the life of the piece and the reactions to it after it leaves our studio.

What I hoped to achieve (motivation?) was a chronicle of a time and place born of my personal history—single and sailing free in another medium, the ocean—the illusive atmosphere and freedom that time allowed me to experience, before marriage, children, and methodical living.

So I'd have to answer that I hope to achieve sharing my freedom through the trespass of art.

AWARDS:
3rd Place
Innovative Pieced, Professional
1989

Collection of The National Quilt Museum

Tradition, authenticity, quality, and precision define the artistry and achievement Rose seeks in her quiltmaking.

CROWN OF CERISE
94" x 94", Rose Sanders, Harahan, LA, 1986. Cottons; hand appliquéd and hand quilted with trapunto.
1997.07.05

ROSE SANDERS

JANE SASSAMAN

Jane celebrates the energy and beauty of nature, especially plant life, in her work. She teaches others to nurture creativity, observe more closely, and how to overcome creative obstacles.

TREE OF LIFE: SPRING
69.5" x 78.5", Jane Sassaman, Harvard, IL, 1994. Cottons; machine appliquéd, pieced, and quilted.
2007.02.01

AWARDS:
1st Place
Wall Quilt, Professional
1995

*B*eing true to herself and listening to her creative soul guides Sharon's quiltmaking. She considers herself a teacher first, then a quiltmaker.

FLOWER OF LIFE

87" x 87", Sharon Schamber, Payson, AZ, 2007. Cottons; macine pieced and appliquéd, longarm machine quilted.
2007.05.01

AWARDS:
Hancock's of Paducah
Best of Show
2007

SHARON SCHAMBER

SHARON SCHAMBER

SEDONA ROSE
105" x 110", Sharon Schamber, Payson, AZ, 2006. Cottons, Swarovski® crystals; machine pieced and appliquéd, longarm machine quilted.
2006.03.01

AWARDS:
Hancock's of Paducah
Best of Show
2006

Elsie draws on family and cultural influences when making her quilts. Color, pattern scale, and quilting design combine to make her quilts successful.

AMISH MUTUAL AID
75" x 83", Elsie Schlabach, Millersburg, OH, 1993. Cottons; machine pieced, hand pieced, and hand quilted.
1997.07.01

ELSIE SCHLABACH

CYNTHIA SCHMITZ

Machine quilting combines with color, fabric, sewing, and problem solving in Cynthia's quilts.

BLUEBERRY MORNING
85" x 85", Cynthia Schmitz, Arlington Heights, IL, 2002. Cottons, monofilament nylon thread; machine pieced, trapuntoed, and machine quilted.
2003.02.01

AWARDS:
Bernina
Machine Workmanship
2003

I know people do connect with my quilts, but I can't say why.

I like to think it's because I haven't strayed too far from tradition. I'm a use-what-you-have, create-from-scraps, repeated-geometric-pattern kind of quilter.

Like legions of women before me, I like the challenge, the structure, the utility, and the artistry of quiltmaking.

I love to see the delight in the eyes of others as they view my work. Each new quilt is tangible evidence that I am content doing what I do, which, I assume, is the goal of every artist.

PROSPERITY

84" x 84", Elaine M. Seaman, Kalamazoo, MI, 1985. Cottons; hand pieced, machine pieced, and hand quilted.
1997.06.59

ELAINE M. SEAMAN

JUDY HENDREY SEIDEL

I don't make quilts for art's sake; I do make them for heart's sake.

I selfishly achieve great satisfaction from designing quilts, choosing fabric, playing with it, hand quilting it, and seeing how the quilt turns out.

I don't know if I'm scattered or eclectic, but I get my inspiration from many directions. My greatest achievement occurs when a person turns up who loves one of my quilts and then it becomes theirs.

I'm a person who would be making quilts no matter where I happened to be or what might be going on around me—I make quilts because I can't help but do so. They give me great joy and I have the feeling that others delight in them also.

HEARTS & STARS
40" x 48", Judy Seidel, Ft. Collins, CO, 1984. Cottons and cotton blends; hand and machine pieced, hand quilted.
1997.06.28

My ultimate hope is that others will feel joy and be inspired when viewing my quilts.

Since making JAVANESE JUNGLE in 1988 I've had many opportunities to work with quilters of all skill levels. It has been a rewarding journey sharing my ideas and methods in the hopes of enhancing their enthusiasm for quilts and art in general.

For me, quilting is more than a hobby. It is something I do every day—often all day. It is my passion.

I wish for everyone a passion of that degree in their lives.

When showing my art quilts in public venues, classes, and programs, my goal is always to bring pleasure and inspiration to the viewer.

AWARDS:
First Place
Appliqué, Amateur
1988

AUDREE L. SELLS

JAVANESE JUNGLE
75" x 94", Audree L. Sells, Chaska, MN, 1988. Cottons; hand pieced, hand appliquéd, hand embroidered and beaded, and hand quilted.
1992.16.01

POLLY SEPULVADO

GRANDMOTHER'S ENGAGEMENT RING
76" x 94", Polly Sepulvado, M.D., Roseburg, OR, 1986. Cottons; hand appliquéd, machine pieced, and hand quilted.
1997.06.27

I continue to be passionate about quilting after 32 years.

I work full-time but make time to quilt "a little" every day. I have the luxury of a large quilt room and can walk away and leave a project at any point and return whenever I can. Usually there are more than a dozen projects going at once.

I'm enthusiastic about learning new techniques and styles. Although I have challenged myself to make wallhangings, I really like making bed quilts. They are used by my family and I enjoy displaying my quilts at my office.

I suppose what I want to accomplish with my quilt artistry is to satisfy my own creative desires and to try to please others with my work.

AWARDS:
Third Place
Traditional Patchwork, Amateur
1986

Collection of The National Quilt Museum

*P*ragmatism and a passing fancy with quiltmaking have defined Jonathan's artistry.

AIR SHOW
81" x 81", Jonathan Shannon, Phoenix, AZ, 1992. Cottons; machine pieced, hand appliquéd, couched cording, and hand quilted. Named one of the 100 Best American Quilts of the 20th Century. 1996.01.01

AWARDS:
AQS
Best of Show
1993

JONATHON SHANNON

MARION SHENK

A lifetime of quilting has been a seamless artistic experience for Marion.

SHADOW BALTIMORE BRIDE
86" x 102", Marion Shenk, Scottdale, PA, 1986. Cotton broadcloth, voile, and cotton embroidery floss; hand quilted by various quilters at maker's quilt shop. 1997.06.70

AWARDS:
Third Place
Other Techniques, Professional
1986

Traditional patterns used in unusual ways, color, fabric selection and use, and hand quilting are the challenges Virginia finds most exciting and satisfying in quiltmaking.

SAMARKAND
80.5" x 81", Virginia Siciliano, Lebanon, PA, 2001. Cottons; machine pieced, hand quilted.
2007.11.01

AWARDS:
Third Place
Traditional Pieced, Amateur
2001

VIRGINIA SICILIANO

JUDY SIMMONS

The drive to become a fiber artist was greatly influenced by my family who made everything with their sewing machines.

I work intuitively, pulling inspiration from the things I love such as old family pictures and papers, textured rocks, peeling paint and crumbling stones on sidewalks and buildings, things that have endured the elements of time, interesting but not necessarily beautiful. I am also inspired by the beautiful colors and textures of nature.

My camera is always with me, ready to capture these wonderful things. This imagery is printed, embellished, and combined with other surface design techniques to create a unique piece.

NOSEGAY
36" diameter, Judy Simmons, Marietta, GA, 1986. Cottons; hand appliquéd (including *broderie perse*) and hand quilted.
1997.06.47

Before she passed away, Martha was one of America's best-known quilters. She is remembered by friends as a teacher and mentor for those in the craft.

CHIPS AND WHETSTONES
80" x 89.5", Martha B. Skelton, Vicksburg, MS, 1987. Cottons; hand and machine pieced, hand appliquéd, and hand quilted. 1992.02.01

MARTHA B. SKELTON

MARTHA B. SKELTON

NEW YORK BEAUTY
*77" x 90", Martha B. Skelton, Vicksburg,
MS, 1986. Cottons; hand pieced, machine
pieced, and hand quilted.
1997.06.44*

AWARDS:
*First Place
Tradtional Pieced, Professional
1987*

194

Collection of The National Quilt Museum

Ruth's lifelong involvement in several art forms, including painting, sculpture, and jewelry making, built the foundation for her quiltmaking.

SQUARE WITHIN A SQUARE WITHIN A SQUARE WITHIN A SQUARE
102" x 102", Ruth Britton Smalley, Houston, TX, 1986. Cottons; machine pieced and hand quilted.
1997.08.01

AWARDS:
Third Place
Theme: Log Cabin
1987

FRASER SMITH

FLOATING

65" x 42" x 4", is a solid wood sculpture by Fraser Smith, Tampa, FL. Appearing to be softly draped over a rope, the folds of Fraser's hanging quilt fool the eye. Tiny indentations mimic quilting stitches, but at more than 80 pounds this carved solid wood sculpture is anything but wrap-around cuddly.

I make trompe l'oeil wood sculptures of items made of fabric or leather. My subject matter is drawn from things that we tend to save or cherish even after they are no longer useful—items we might want to keep simply for the memories they hold.

Like all trompe l'oeil artists, I'm trying to challenge the viewer, but I want to take it beyond the simple mastery of technique.

In my quilt works, I'm attempting to combine good design and color use with an interesting but unexpected object.

I want the viewer to initially feel that it's a bit "out of place." I want them to think, "Well, that's interesting, but why is it there?" When they discover it's wood, they have to reevaluate.

Collection of The National Quilt Museum

Since the very first day of my quiltmaking journey, I have been passionately devoted to teaching the art of creativity and originality in quiltmaking and to making quilts that reflect my deepest feelings and record my most precious memories.

In this endeavor I have strayed from the historic path and played with nontraditional materials and techniques.

My goal has been to help students develop a basic foundation of skills that they can adapt and use as they pursue their individual artistic goals.

When skill and artistic energy ignite, the world is a more beautiful place.

AWARDS:
*Third Place
Traditional Patchwork,
Professional*
1986

LOIS T. SMITH

SPRINGTIME SAMPLER
108" x 108," Lois T. Smith, Rockville, MD, 1986. Cottons, rayon thread; machine pieced and machine quilted.
1997.06.72

NANCY ANN SOBEL

DAWN SPLENDOR
94" x 94", Nancy Ann Sobel, Brooktondale, NY, 1991. Cottons; machine pieced, hand appliquéd, and hand quilted.
1996.01.08

I hope to inspire others to become confident and respectful of their own personal artistic vision.

I also hope to leave a legacy to my future generations that artistry is a wonderful gift and to "Be sure that each one is doing his very best, for then he will have the personal satisfaction of work well done, and won't need to compare himself with someone else." (Galatians 6:4).

Let the work of your hands be guided by what is in your mind and heart.

AWARDS:
AQS
Best of Show
1991

Collection of The National Quilt Museum

A Midwinter Night's Dream

99" x 99", Nancy Ann Sobel, Brooktondale, NY, 1988. Cottons; machine pieced, hand appliquéd, and hand quilted.
1996.01.17

AWARDS:
Gingher
Hand Workmanship
1990

NANCY ANN SOBEL

JUDY SOGN

Quiltmaking in all its forms, including appreciating the work of others, is at the heart of Judy's approach to her art.

STARBURST
95" x 95", Judy Sogn, Seattle, WA, 1990.
Cottons, over-dyed cottons; machine pieced and hand quilted.
1997.06.75

AWARDS:
Second Place
Traditional Pieced, Professional
1991

I enjoy quilting because it is a fulfilling part of my life, and I find it very relaxing.

I am fearful that it is becoming a lost art, as young people become more involved in technology and less involved in handmade crafts.

I hope that the care I put into my quilting, including my intricate stitching and handmade wax thread, will inspire others to take the time to learn this art and take pride in it.

QUILTED COUNTERPANE
72" x 100", Patricia Spadaro, Delmar, NY, 1985. Polished cotton; hand quilted.
1997.06.60

AWARDS:
Second Place
Other Techniques, Amateur
1986

PATRICIA SPADARO

DOREEN SPECKMANN

*I*nnovation, creativity, and humor infused every aspect of Doreen's life, including her quilts.

THE BLADE

62" x 84", Doreen Speckmann, Madison, WI, 1985. Cottons; hand pieced and hand quilted. 1997.06.06

AWARDS:
First Place
Patchwork, Professional
1985

Early in her life, quilts were but a necessary chore for Louise. Later, they became fun, and a way to reveal her playful nature.

COLONIAL LADY

86" x 99½", Louise Stafford, Brewerton, WA, 1984. Cotton and cotton blends; hand pieced, hand appliquéd, hand embroidered, and hand quilted.
1997.07.04

LOUISE STAFFORD

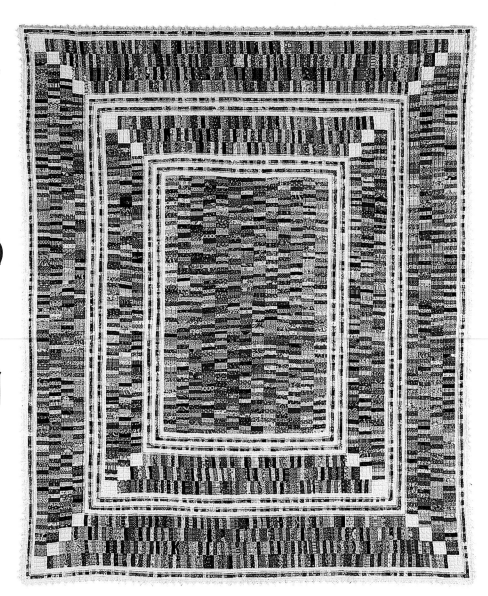

WASTE NOT, WANT NOT
79" x 91", Louise Stafford, Bremerton, WA,
1990. Cottons, cotton blends, lace; machine
pieced and hand quilted.
1992.04.01

204

The combined satisfactions of meticulous hand workmanship and finishing a quilt give Aileen her sense of artistry and achievement.

BALTIMORE REMEMBERED
83" x 103", Aileen Stannis, Berkley, MI, 1996. Cottons; hand appliquéd, hand pieced, and hand quilted.
1996.03.01

AWARDS:
*Gingher
Hand Workmanship
1996*

AILEEN STANNIS

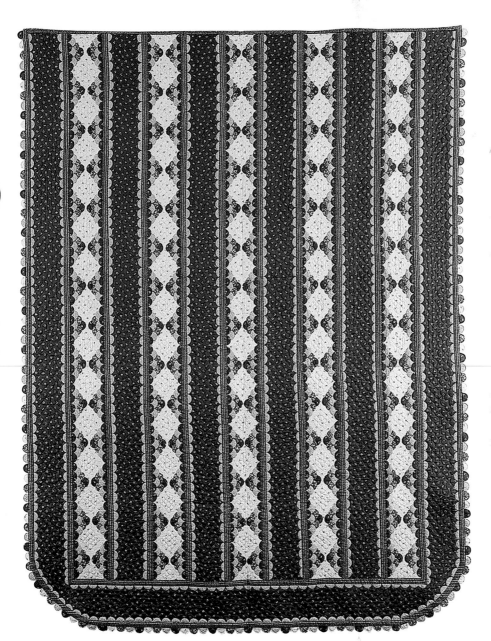

ARLENE STATZ

While she was alive, having two quilts in The National Quilt Museum (then MAQS) was a source of pride and joy for Arlene.

CLAMSHELL
84" x 104", Arlene Statz, Sun Prairie, WI, 1984. Cottons; hand appliquéd, machine pieced, and hand quilted.
1997.06.11

**GRANDMOTHER'S
ENGAGEMENT RING**
74" x 96", Arlene Statz, Sun Prairie, WI,
1986. Cottons; machine pieced, hand appliquéd, and hand quilted.
1997.06.26

ARLENE STATZ

CAROLE STEINER

*T*he primary value of quilting for Carole is how quilting brings women together in a sisterhood.

LILIES ARE FOREVER

76" x 88", Carole Steiner, Santa Maria, CA, 1994. Cottons; machine pieced, hand appliquéd, and hand quilted.
1996.01.15

AWARDS:
Gingher
Hand Workmanship
1995

Faith, color, and devotion to her sister have framed Joyce's quilting achievements.

CELEBRATION
46" x 46", Joyce Stewart, Rexburg, ID, 1988. Cotton; machine pieced and machine quilted.
1992.11.01

JOYCE STEWART

SPLENDOR OF THE RAJAHS
84" x 106", Joyce Stewart, Rexburg, ID, 1985. Cottons; machine pieced and hand quilted. Pattern from *Curves Unlimited* by Joyce M. Schlotzhauer. 1997.06.71

I learned how to piece a Nine Patch when I was nine, but didn't take up quilting in earnest until an accident left me in a full body cast.

I am no longer able to do much quilting, especially on large quilts, due to bad eyesight and arthritis in my hands and back, but I still try to make baby quilts for the young mothers at my work and church for their new babies.

PEACE AND LOVE
96" x 92", Frances Stone, Mayfield, KY, 1985. Cottons, lace, and ribbon; shadow appliqué, hand quilted with embroidery thread.
1997.06.54

FRANCES STONE

ELAINE STONEBRAKER

The dimension achievable in quiltmaking is the source of Elaine's sense of artistry.

RISING MOONS
73" x 67", Elaine Stonebraker, Scottsdale, AZ, 1988. Cottons; hand pieced and hand quilted.
1997.06.64

AWARDS:
Second Place
Pictorial Wall Quilt
1989

Dorothy Mackley
STOVALL

The quality Dorthy seeks in her quiltmaking comes to her better via handwork than machine work.

STAR BRIGHT
81" x 96", Dorothy Mackley Stovall, Livingston, MT, 1985. Cottons; hand pieced and hand quilted.
1997.06.74

JANICE STREETER

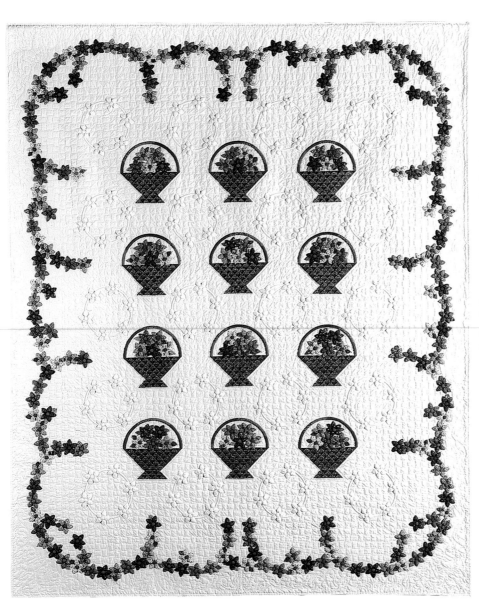

Expressing her individuality is at the core of Janice's quiltmaking artistry and achievement.

SPRING FLOWER BASKETS
88" x 103", Janice Streeter, Virginia Beach, VA, 1989. Cottons; machine pieced, hand appliquéd, and hand quilted. National Quilting Association Masterpiece Quilt. 1996.01.23

AWARDS:
*Gingher
Hand Workmanship*
1989

Collection of The National Quilt Museum

I retired from serious quilting many years ago. I attend quilt conferences several times a year and enjoy seeing the work others are doing and visiting with old friends.

I produce five or six quilts per year. These I give to children, grandchildren, friends, and charity.

I love my hobby. The challenges keep me involved and vital.

CELEBRATION OF AUTUMN
86" x 86", Karmen Streng, Davis, CA, 1985. Cottons; machine pieced and hand quilted.
1992.18.01

AWARDS:
Second Place
Innovative Patchwork, Amateur
1986

MARIE STURMER

*M*arie's approach to quilt-making comes from her formal art training and then a lifetime of teaching art, which required her to adapt many artistic skills and techniques. Painted stencil quilts are her trademark.

RIBBONS AND ROSES
72" x 86", Marie Sturmer, Traverse City, MI, 1989. Cotton; stenciled, hand embroidered, and hand quilted.
1997.06.63

Collection of The National Quilt Museum

Being prolific, having fun with color, entering shows, and seeing her sense of humor evidenced in fabric are the basic tenets of quiltmaking achievement for Patricia.

PETROGLYPH

66" x 79", Patricia L. Styring, St. Augustine, FL, 1997. Cottons, metallic acrylic paint, fabric paint, bleach discharge; machine pieced, appliquéd, and quilted.
2006.01.01

AWARDS:
First Place
Mixed Techniques, Professional
1998

EILEEN BAHRING SULLIVAN

The precision in Eileen's work comes from technique. The designs and colors come from nature. She believes that there is an artist inside each one of us.

WHEN GRANDMOTHER'S LILY GARDEN BLOOMS

62" x 82", Eileen Bahring Sullivan, Alpharetta, GA, 1990. Cottons and blends, hand-dyed fabrics; machine pieced, hand embroidered, and hand quilted. 1997.06.91

AWARDS:
First Place
Innovative Pieced, Professional
1990

Teaching and designing give Sherry distinct senses of accomplishment in her quiltmaking.

INDIAN SUMMER
106" x 106," Sherry Sunday, New Kingston, PA, 1993. Cottons; machine pieced, appliquéd, and quilted.
1997.07.13

GABRIELLE SWAIN

As an artist working in a variety of media, when I discovered quiltmaking, all my needs were satisfied. Painting, photography, and graphic design all seemed a perfect fit for quilts.

After going through many stages, appliqué became my favorite technique. With this technique, almost any design could be accomplished.

Since that time, the majority of my work is centered on nature. Believing in the principle of working from where you live, almost all my work is inspired by the landscapes in Texas.

Celebrating nature as a part of who we are in instead of separate from us will continue to be the focus of my work.

Hopefully, the work will do justice to the beauty outside my door.

A lifelong fascination with all things needle and thread led up to Deborah's passion for making quilts.

MARINER'S COMPASS
78" x 90", Deborah Warren Techentin, Dunnellon, FL, 1985. Cottons; machine and hand pieced and hand quilted. 1997.06.38

BARBARA TEMPLE

Barbara has preferred making picture quilts from the start of her quilting life, likening the process of creating depth and dimension in fabric to painting.

VOICE OF FREEDOM
66" x 65", Barbara Temple, Mesa, AZ, 1987. Cottons; hand appliquéd and hand quilted.
1997.06.90

Exploring design and color anew with each quilt she made was the heart of Joyce's artistry. In her lifetime, achievement came about by carrying on the tradition through teaching others and judging.

NIGHT AND NOON VARIATION
72" x 92", Joyce Ann Tennery, Oak Ridge, TN, 1987. Cottons; hand pieced and hand quilted.
1997.06.45

JOYCE ANN TENNERY

LEURETA BEAM THIEME

Leureta found self-expression through sewing clothes and creating original clothing designs, and quiltmaking has served as another artistic outlet.

ORIENTAL POPPY
90" x 95", Leureta Beam Thieme, Pasadena, MD, 1987. Polished cottons; machine pieced, hand appliquéd, and hand quilted.
1997.06.51

For more than thirty years I have been interested in textile art. Along with a lifelong interest in history, I developed a special interest in quilts.

By combining piecing, applique, and quilting by hand, I take inspiration from earlier works to evolve my own designs, using traditional techniques I continue to refine. I am especially interested in appliqué because it allows me to freely create and express my ideas in new designs. I prefer hand quilting because it allows fine control of my work.

I enjoy teaching and take great satisfaction as many of my students progress to become accomplished quilters.

My vision is to create new and unique quilts by interpreting vintage works and incorporating combinations of design elements and color layering.

AWARDS:
AQS
Best of Show
1997

JUDITH THOMPSON

VINTAGE ROSE GARDEN
94" x 94.5", Judith Thompson, Wenonah, NJ, 1996. Cottons, new and vintage; hand appliquéd, hand pieced, and hand quilted.
1997.04.01

ZENA THORPE

ALABASTER RELIEF
74" x 86", Zena Thorpe, Chatsworth, CA, 2003. Cotton sateen, rayon thread, wool batting; hand appliquéd, embroidered, and quilted.
2005.01.01

*W*illiam Morris, founder of The Arts and Crafts Movement, believed in integrated creativity and labor.

He said, "That thing which I understand by real art is the expression by man of his pleasure in labor." He argued ceaselessly that there must be satisfaction of creation in the labor that produces goods.

This is a philosophy to which I subscribe and which expresses my hope for achievement in my quiltmaking: the personal satisfaction and pleasure that come from creating something with my heart and hands.

If that something is a piece of art which gives pleasure to others, then that satisfaction is multiplied tenfold.

AWARDS:
AQS
Hand Workmanship
2005

Collection of The National Quilt Museum

I constantly strive to create work that is aesthetically pleasing and that exemplifies the traditions that are historically present in quiltmaking, holding myself to a high standard of workmanship to achieve this.

In pursuit of my quilting craft, I have attempted to create designs that are appealing to the traditional side of quilting but still have characteristics that are reflective of contemporary quilts. When I'm designing things that are traditional, I want them to have a contemporary flair and often use color to accomplish this. I hope that my work honors quilters from centuries past and provides a bridge between the two.

AWARDS:
*Bernina
Machine Workmanship*
2006

RICKY TIMS

FIRE DRAGON RHAPSODY

60" x 60", Ricky Tims, LaVeta, CO, 2004. Hand-dyed cottons, metallic threads; raw-edge and fusible machine appliqué, trapunto, machine quilted.
2006.05.01

MARJORIE D. TOWNSEND

Marjorie's use of quiltmaking as an art form was based on years of quilting as a fundamental necessity.

TULIPS IN A BASKET
87" x 108", Marjorie D. Townsend, Parsons, TN, 1984. Cottons; hand appliquéd and hand quilted.
1997.06.87

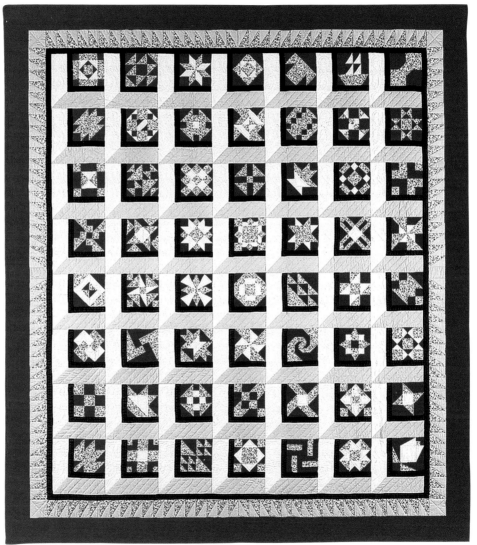

The members of this Cadiz, Kentucky, area quilt guild meet regularly, take trips together, conduct community service projects, and volunteer at The National Quilting Museum.

TRADITION IN THE ATTIC
86.5" x 94.5", Trigg Co. Quilters, Cadiz, KY, 1988. Cottons; hand pieced and hand quilted.
2000.05.01

LUDMILA USPENSKAYA

As an academically trained artist and designer, I have always created artworks based on my own experiences, surroundings, and ideas.

The artistry of my quilt-making explores the capacity of my creativity and brings quilt-making to the level of high art.

TRADITIONAL BOUQUET
52" x 66", Ludmila Uspenskaya, New York, NY, 1995. Cottons; machine appliquéd and machine quilted.
1995.01.01

I quilt because I love fabric in its many colors and patterns, and I love cutting it up and sewing it back together to make new designs.

Even though I always said I had no artistic talent (translation: ability to draw) and avoided art classes every time I could, I think, deep in my heart, this is what I always longed to be able to do.

I make quilts for enjoyment, both mine and others'. If I like a quilt when it is finished, I am happy. If others like it, too, I am happier.

AMISH EASTER BASKETS
84" x 110", Elsie Vredenburg, Tustin, MI, 1987. Cottons; machine pieced and hand quilted.
1992.14.01

AWARDS:
Third Place
Theme: Baskets
1988

ELSIE VREDENBURG

ELSIE VREDENBURG

ICE FANTASIA
74" x 87", Elsie Vredenburg, Tustin, MI, 1989. Cottons; machine pieced and hand quilted.
1992.10.01

AWARDS:
Second Place
Theme: Fans
1990

Collection of The National Quilt Museum

I made my first quilt from maternity blouse scraps and children's play clothes, which filled three large grocery bags.

Then I made a quilt for each of our four beds, my brother, sister, and parents.

Next I made two quilts to keep myself busy while my husband was in Vietnam for a year.

After that I discovered quilt shops and all manner of wonderful things just for quilters like classes from all the great quilting teachers, non-juried and juried quilt shows, and publications.

Now, I want to use up my fabric and make all my design sketches and finish up my latest quilt (with my 95-year-old mother) and have the good grace to give some of these quilts away. They're taking up every closet!

CAROL WADLEY

SUNSET KITES
63" x 63", Carol Wadley, Hillsboro, OR, 1985. Cottons; machine pieced and hand quilted.
1997.06.80

DEBRA WAGNER

One of the early proponents of machine quilting, Debra's trademark achievement in the quilting world has been precision machine work.

FLORAL URNS
90" x 90", Debra Wagner, Cosmos, MN, 1992. Cottons; machine pieced, machine appliquéd, machine embroidered, and machine quilted.
1996.01.11

AWARDS:
Bernina
Machine Workmanship
1993

OHIO BRIDE'S QUILT
81" x 81", Debra Wagner, Cosmos, MN, 1989. Cottons; machine pieced and machine quilted with trapunto. 1997.06.49

AWARDS:
First Place Other Techniques
Viewers' Choice
1990

DEBRA WAGNER

DEBRA WAGNER

SUNBURST QUILT
90" x 89", Debra Wagner, Cosmos, MN, 1994. Cottons; machine pieced and machine quilted with trapunto. 1996.01.25

AWARDS:
*Bernina
Machine Workmanship*
1995

In the short period of time Deborah was a quilter before her death, she embraced machine appliqué and quilting techniques and developed a signature style in an impressive body of work for one so young.

NIGHT FLOWERS
60" x 60", Deborah Lynn Ward, Arroyo Grande, CA, 1990. Cottons; machine pieced, machine appliquéd, hand beaded, and machine quilted.
1992.19.01

DEBORAH LYNN WARD

BREEZE
55" x 43.5", Rachel Wetzler, St. Charles, IL, 2006. Cottons, polyester sheer, Prismacolor art pencils, Setacdor paints, paint markers, beads, fusible web and interfacing; machine pieced, appliquéd, and quilted; hand embroidered and beaded.
2007.09.01

To safely cross the street, children are taught three words: stop, look, and listen. An exceptional quilt achieves the same three things.

A quilt with strong visual impact stops people in their tracks.

As the viewer looks closely at the quilt, the complexity of design and attention to detail becomes apparent.

If a person takes the time to listen, the quilt will speak to them—sometimes with enough impact to alter their life in some way.

My goal is to honor God by creating quilts that help the viewer stop, look, and listen.

My hope is that they will see and hear beauty and truth.

AWARDS:
Moda
Best Wall Quilt
2007

Collection of The National Quilt Museum

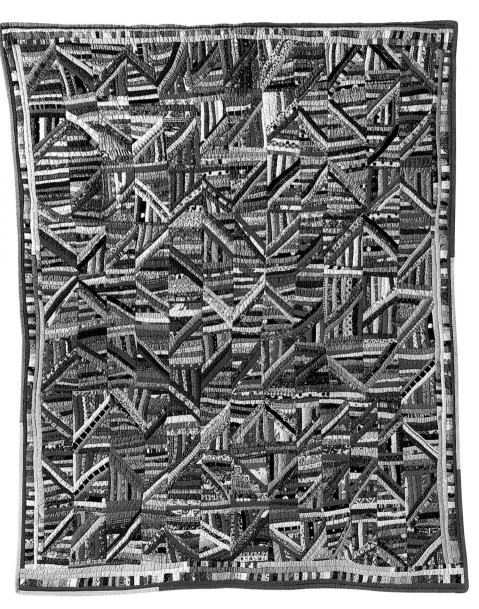

That Anna's improvisational approach to making quilts has unintentionally influenced other quiltmakers surprises her, and what pleases her is that her art is something others enjoy.

A LI'L BIT CRAZY TWO
63" x 78", Anna Williams, Baton Rouge, LA, 1994; quilted by Mary Walker. Cottons; hand and machine pieced and hand quilted.
2001.09.01

ANNA WILLIAMS

Beverly Mannisto
WILLIAMS

Hand quilting gave Beverly a way to express her desire to create lasting works of creativity and artistry.

VICTORIAN FANTASY OF FEATHERS AND LACE
89" x 104", Beverly Mannisto Williams, Cadillac, MI, 1986. Cotton, handmade bobbin lace edge; hand quilted. National Quilting Association Masterpiece Quilt. 1996.01.29

AWARDS:
Gingher
Hand Workmanship
1987

The majority of my quilts depict realistic wildlife and include some traditional piecing.

Having a deep appreciation of traditional quilting, I try to display an area of piecing within my design. However, I'm first and last an artist who needs to create an original work of art.

Working with today's tremendous selection of fabrics stimulates the imagination and makes the creative juices flow.

I hope to pass along my love of animals and inspire others to appreciate their beauty through my work.

By the end of my quilting days, I hope to have inspired a number of quilters to expand their talents to include not only traditional quilts, but other forms of the art.

AWARDS:
*Best Quilt Lewis and Clark
Expedition Quilts
Nashville, Tennessee*
2003

Collection of The National Quilt Museum

CASSANDRA WILLIAMS

THE MAP MAKERS
56.5" x 65", Cassandra Williams, Grants Pass, OR, 2003. Cottons; raw-edge machine appliqué; machine quilted, hand painted and beaded.
2004.03.01

JUANITA GIBSON YEAGER

LILIES OF AUTUMN

70" x 74", Juanita Gibson Yeager, Louisville, KY, 1991. Cottons; hand pieced and hand quilted.
1997.06.32

What I hope to achieve with the artistry of my quiltmaking is to convey successfully, through the use of shapes abstracted from nature, my love and fascination with color and cloth.

Underlying the bold, large-scale graphic nature of my work is my use of colors that have both seasonal connotations and cultural undertones. I hope I have mastered this aspect of my art well enough that it shows in my work.

Because I consider myself an artist, I want those who see my work to feel my joy and sense my happiness.

To a lesser degree, I want people to see my love of cloth and my respect for the traditional quilts that covered our beds long before they graced our walls.

Quilts are items of intense passion in our lives and tug at our heartstrings like few other things.

At birth, we are swaddled in a quilt. As a child, we have a "security" quilt. When we get married, we are given a wedding quilt. When we are sick and dying, we are comforted by a quilt.

We can take a trip down memory lane by standing in front of a quilt that carries us back to days of our childhood.

Quilts provide a vehicle for me to inspire our generation to achieve all they can, and to leave a part of myself behind as a visual reminder for future generations of a passion that runs deep in my life and defines who I am.

AWARDS:
*Bernina
Machine Workmanship*
2007

BUCKSKIN
78" x 79", Marla Yeager, Ava, MO, 2006. Cottons, hand-dyed cottons, silk thread, nylon monofilament thread; machine pieced.
2007.07.01

LOUISE YOUNG

SILVERSWORD – DEGENER'S DREAM
97" x 97", Louise Young, Tioga, PA, 1988. Cottons; hand appliquéd and hand quilted.
MAQS 1992.06.01

My work has been influenced by indigenous cultures which produce textiles that are not only beautiful, but utilitarian, designed to incorporate art in everyday life.

My goal is to create something decorative and functional. All of my quilts are designed to be used on a bed to provide warmth.

In addition, I emphasize natural products in both the raw materials (batting, fabric, thread) and the tools that I use. Since cotton is one of the most chemically intensive agricultural products in the world, whenever possible, I use organically grown cotton that has been dyed with natural or low-impact dyes.

In this way, I hope that my quilts will not only provide warmth for this generation but for healthy generations in the future.

AWARDS:
First Place
Appliqué, Amateur
1989

Collection of The National Quilt Museum

An inherited love of quilting from her mother and grand-mother and the opportunity to devote a lot of time to quilting afforded through long winters in the Big Horn Mountains fueled the late Nadene's artistry and achievements.

STAINED GLASS WINDOWS
98" x 112", Nadene Zowada, Buffalo, WY, 1983. Cotton/polyester; hand appliquéd and quilted.
1997.06.73

NADENE ZOWADA

INDEX

MUSEUM ACTIVITIES

The Museum offers several activities to motivate children to get involved in quilting.

Unique and beautiful gifts are in abundance at the Museum gift shop.

Workshops are offered by some of the most notable people in quilting.

Stained glass windows featured in the Museum lobby.